Men and women worked together to
build their little houses. The method was
invariable: they built one room and they
lived in it until they built another room.

John Steinbeck, on Ukrainian houses,
A Russian Journal, **1948**

In memory of
Vera, Viktor, and Lyusia

SUMMER KITCHENS

RECIPES AND REMINISCENCES
FROM EVERY CORNER OF UKRAINE

Olia Hercules

Photography by Elena Heatherwick & Joe Woodhouse

weldon**owen**

Contents

The summer kitchen

This cookbook is not just about cooking in the summer. It is about a very special place, the perfect prism through which to look at Ukraine's culinary culture in all its regional, climatic, and seasonal diversity.

I grew up in the south of Ukraine, in a small town called Kakhovka. Apart from having a regular kitchen indoors, we had something else: a separate little house, nothing glamorous – just a one-room brick structure, which we called *litnya kuhnia*, "summer kitchen." It was situated in our courtyard, closer to the place where we grew our fruit and vegetables, and was a natural and unremarkable part of our lives.

I live in London now, with hardly any space for a shed, let alone a summer kitchen, but the memory of having a separate cooking-workshop space makes me feel as though back then we had more luxury than we thought. It was only when I very casually mentioned summer kitchens to my friends here that I realized they were actually a bit of a phenomenon, quite idiosyncratic and magical. I was suddenly burning to find out more about this tradition. Little did I know that the summer kitchen's story would turn out to be even more interesting than I could have imagined.

To clarify, these were more than the outside spaces you find in some hot countries, where people cook al fresco under an awning. They were separate buildings with the main purpose of being a kitchen. People cooked and ate there all summer, and sometimes used them to prepare bigger feasts in winter as well, especially during festivities.

Summer kitchens probably started as an extension of dugout barns called *zemlyanky*, where animals were kept and people sometimes lived as well. Some of the ones I visited were largely unchanged from the

>>

day they were built. The materials they were made of varied from region to region, from brick and shell rock in the south, to wood or clay in central and northwestern Ukraine. The local names changed too: they were known as *budka* (cabin) in southeastern Besarabia and *shopa* (barn) in northwestern areas.

The reason summer kitchens exist at all is because of the climate. Ukraine is often associated with Russia, and has a reputation for being cold, snowy, and harsh. But it is also huge, with a wide range of climates. And in summer, which I remember coming early during my childhood, we would often say that it was hot enough to "crack the flagstones" – *asfalt repayetsa*, in the local dialect.

Warmed by the blazing sun and ancient humus, Ukrainian soil is some of the most fertile in the world. Called *chornozem*, "black soil," it has also been known as black gold. In the 1940s, the Nazis allegedly attempted to transport trainloads of this precious soil to Germany, and since the 1990s, following the breakup of the Soviet Union, it has become a black market commodity.

In the years after World War II, when things were improving slightly, the following scenario became common. Imagine a scorching-hot Ukrainian summer in the mid-1950s. A young couple would get married. What made sense for them to do, especially in rural areas, was to start with a small building, containing a makeshift bed and a kerosene stove – it was both a bedroom and a place where the meals were cooked. Sometimes a couple might already have children by the time they acquired land of their own, so the whole family would stay in this bedroom-kitchen. If there was a craftsman in the village, a large masonry oven called a *pich* would be built into it.

Their whole life and livelihood would sprout up like mushrooms around this modest structure. Normally it would take six warm months to build the main house, sometimes a year or even longer. During this time, the couple would be planting an orchard and a vegetable patch too. They wouldn't always work on their own. People in the village,

sometimes as many as fifty, would come and help out, bringing hay to construct the walls of the *khata* (Ukrainian clay and straw house), singing as they went. All they asked for in return was some lunch and dinner, and perhaps a similar favor in the future. Once the main house was completed, the family would move there, and the small, interim house would become the summer kitchen.

When my mother was a child, in the early 1960s, my grandparents bought a three-bedroom house. The summer kitchen, an essential feature in their eyes, was missing, so my grandfather Viktor decided to add it on, as an annex to the main house. But just near the very spot where it felt most natural to build it was a mature yellow cherry tree, and one of the main branches, as thick as a thigh, was firmly in the way. Viktor, the gentlest man, loved the tree so much that he could not imagine cutting this branch off.

What he did next was extraordinary: he simply built the branch into the kitchen's structure. So there was this massive tree branch going right through one of the walls and sticking out of the roof. Now you might think that he must have been an eccentric kind of guy to tackle this mad and dubious construction maneuver. But in my travels around Ukraine I have discovered other families with equally quirky summer kitchens, born of a similar ethos – it seems to me that the underlying intention is to try and live in harmony with nature, with gratitude to the land and what it gives you. Summer kitchens encourage a very intimate, almost spiritual connection to everything living around you.

Remember that, during my grandfather's day, we were still in the Soviet Union. And even though I was the child of 1980s *perestroyka*, which heralded big changes, I still remember empty shops and long lines to pay the electricity bill or buy mayonnaise (a collective obsession). But unlike people in Moscow and other cities, who had little opportunity to grow their own produce, rural Ukrainians were able to nurture a way of life that historically had served them best – husbandry. So at the time

>>

a summer kitchen was not just some romantic idea, as it might have become now. It symbolized the core, the backbone of life; it was both a place of hard labor and a sanctuary.

Summer kitchens were practical. In summer the heat could be intense and there was rarely any air conditioning, often not even extractor fans. To have a separate place where frying, cooking, and preserving could be done was very handy. Apart from everyday and festive cooking, summer kitchens were where all the Fermenting, pickling, and preserving happened, on an almost industrial scale, come September. Pick your fruit and vegetables by the bucketful, carry them into the summer kitchen, and start the mammoth pickling operation, leaving the doors and windows wide open.

Today, more often than not, people do have air conditioning and extractor fans, and some are using their summer kitchens as dumping grounds for old junk and suitcases, or are simply dismantling them. There is also a desire to clad everything in plastic. I understand that insulation is important when using an outbuilding in winter, but I have seen old, well-made wooden kitchens with masterfully built two-ton *pich* masonry ovens still doing the job they did in the middle of the twentieth century.

And some of these summer kitchens are indeed being turned into winter havens. After the gas crisis of 2009 caused energy prices to soar, a lot of people, especially older couples living on their own, thumbed their nose at the problem, and spent the cold winters in their snug summer kitchens, which were much cheaper to heat.

Whatever the future holds for summer kitchens, I doubt many with a *pich* will survive much longer, although I have met some dedicated young people who are interested in resurrecting their summer kitchens and masonry ovens. And, at least on paper, I am determined to give these practical and dreamy places – and the food traditions and cherished recipes created in them – the attention they deserve.

A taste of Ukraine

Ukraine is a huge country, with a very complex, turbulent and fascinating history. *Ukrayina* means "borderland," and it has indeed been a border province to a number of powerful empires through the centuries. A large swath of Ukrainian territory consists of an open, unprotected, and very fertile corridor of steppes, which is extremely tempting to invaders. As a result, in very simplistic terms, Ukraine's borders have oscillated between Russian, Austrian, Polish, and Turkish rule, with Crimean Tatar and Mongolian invasions in between.

However, despite the lack of recognition of Ukraine as an independent state prior to the breakup of the Soviet Union, the people living on its land have developed their own beautiful, melodic language, and a distinctive culture and cuisine. In her seminal book *European Peasant Cookery*, Elisabeth Luard called Romania "a kind of culinary Galapagos Islands." She was referring to the merging of Nordic influences (as seen in various methods of preservation, including fermentation, fish-drying, and pickling) with an almost Mediterranean use of fresh vegetables and fruit and baking techniques. I feel her description might equally well apply to Ukraine. Sandwiched between Poland and Russia, with Belarus to the north, Romania and Moldova to the southwest, and Turkey a stone's throw away across the Black Sea, Ukraine's regional food is very diverse.

Besides, as its borders have been stretched and pulled, Ukraine has been exposed to plenty of other ethnic, religious, and cultural influences, which have been integrated into its cuisine, making it one of the most exciting food cultures in Europe. Nowadays, you can find Transcarpathian villages where Hungarian,

>>

Slovakian, and Polish dishes live happily alongside the more usual fare of quintessentially Ukrainian borsch and *varenyky*. This mosaic of influences pervades every family. As a friend in Transcarpathia puts it, "My grandmother was born in Czechoslovakia, got married in Hungary, and died in Soviet Ukraine, yet she never left her village."

Both Russia and the Ottoman Empire once encouraged people from neighboring countries, known as *kolonists*, to come and settle in Ukrainian territory. As a result, the southwest of Ukraine is peppered with Bulgarian- and Moldovan-style villages. And in the south, in the region of Kherson, there are also historically German and Swedish settlements. Lviv, in western Ukraine, and Odesa, on the Black Sea coast, as well as the whole region of Bukovina, used to be among the biggest Jewish hubs in Europe. To some extent, these pockets of different cultures remain today, and their heritage still resonates in various local dishes.

In the village of Krynychne, blue-eyed women with bronzed skin, the descendants of Bulgarian *kolonists*, sit at a low table they call a *sini*, rolling out thin dough with special slender rolling pins. The dough is filled with salty cheese and turned into flatbreads reminiscent of the Turkish *gozleme*. The Greek-blue walls of their kitchen are adorned with traditionally embroidered, colorful Ukrainian ritual cloths called *rushnyk*...echoes of Ottoman culture encapsulated in a Ukrainian summer kitchen.

In Crimea and by the Sea of Azov, not too far from where I was born, Tatar people, who returned from exile in Central Asia after the collapse of the USSR, are keeping their own traditions alive – they still make the sour yogurt called *katyk* and heady lamb broths with chickpeas.

In the northwest, in the Carpathian highlands, Hutsul people make rich polenta and potato dishes, essential to sustain their life of hard work in the mountains.

Landscapes vary along with the people: from the deep, dark forests and marshland of Polisia in the north, through the verdant Carpathian hills splattered with deep-yellow hay bales, we descend into the dips of neat valleys with babbling brooks and eventually emerge onto the plateaus and flatlands. The sense of space that the steppes bring, and the sheer expanse of them, brings to mind Ukrainian polyphonic singing – deeply sad, haunting sounds, chasing a limitless skyline.

Of course, the local climate changes with the landscape, and consequently so do ingredients. The northern marshes are full of wild bilberries and lingonberries, sea buckthorn, and wild rose. Eels are still found in the rivers, although their numbers are depleted. The northeastern woodlands of Slobozhanshchyna region are home to pheasant, boar, and hare, and an abundance of chestnuts. In Halychyna, the area surrounding Lviv, the herbs are different from those used in southern Ukraine – it is almost impossible to find fresh coriander (cilantro), but there is plenty of wild thyme and marjoram. And in June, Lviv markets have jars of intensely sweet wild strawberries with fern leaves for a lid.

Carpathian sheep's milk and goat's milk cheeses, such as *vurda* and *brynza*, are the best in the country. How could they not be when the grazing pastures are dense with wild thyme all summer? Transcarpathian honey, diligently made by colonies of the region's distinctive small bees, bursts with the headiness of wild flowers. And corn grows easily up here in the mountains, hence the popularity of polenta-like dishes.

Central Ukraine has a little bit of everything – the gifts of the north, like mushrooms and parsnips, as well as warm, sun-ripened fruit such as pears, peaches, and apricots. Poltava and its surroundings also harbor some of the most interesting fruit-preservation traditions in all of Ukraine.

I may be biased but, for me, the south, with its blazing sun, milder winters, and fertile soil, seems to offer the widest variety of fruit and vegetables. It also has access to the bounty of the Black and Azov seas, including flounders, giant whelks, and the small sweet

>>

fish called gobies; there is also the Dnipro River, which teems with crayfish, zander, carp, and catfish. Gigantic, scarred pink tomatoes are used with abandon. People's gardens boast equally large eggplants, sweet and hot peppers, herbs, rhubarb, prickly cucumbers, and candy-sweet potatoes so flavorsome they need little flavoring once cooked. The long, unpopulated stretches of road between villages are bordered with orchards of red, yellow, and morello cherry trees, quinces, apples, pears, peaches, apricots, and plums. In the towns, great big mulberry trees grow in the streets, their rich black or whitish-pink berries strewn across the pathways in late summer. The herb stall is a small mountain of dill, with its umbrella-like crowns, coriander (cilantro), purple basil, sorrel, green onions, and parsley. It is a cornucopia worthy of an artist's brush.

To the west, in Vylkove, which is billed as the Ukrainian Venice (but I feel is more like the Ukrainian Vietnam, as it's wilder), the waters of the Danube are home to the famous herrings called *dunayka*. Sturgeon is also used, albeit less these days. Fish is sneaked into every iconic Ukrainian dish, from yeasted *pyrizhky* buns and dumplings to borsch.

During the Soviet era, the policy of standardization introduced a handful of standard dishes to Soviet cafeterias, and hence to people's homes. Some regional traditions and even the Ukrainian language itself struggled to survive, especially in the east and some parts of southern Ukraine. Communities in the west were farther away from the Russian border and so were more able to preserve their dialects, rituals, and embroidery and other crafts, as well as their cuisine.

Early-twentieth-century Ukrainian cookbooks, written by western Ukrainian authors, reveal dishes steeped in Austro-Hungarian culture. Also, ingredients like asparagus and artichokes are featured a lot! By the time my parents came along, these ingredients were long forgotten, as they did not produce high enough yields for collectivized farming. Happily, they are now making a comeback, as is people's interest in reviving the old ways. It feels like regionality is also resurgent, with Besarabian and Tatar restaurants in Odesa and Kyiv, and places that specialize in Halychyna food in Lviv.

Ukraine may have had a tough run for almost a thousand years, but the silver lining lies in the richness of its culinary culture – something to be embraced, reveled in, and explored.

Fermenting, pickling, and preserving

THE SEPTEMBER SESSIONS

The beginning of autumn always signaled it was time to preserve and let things "go sour," as we say in Ukraine. Buckets of the sweetest tomatoes, cucumbers, apples, plums, and apricots were brought in through the lace-curtained doorway of the summer kitchen. We children would sit on stumpy wooden stools and pick out the bruised and blemished – only the best, undamaged specimens were to make it into the preserving jars.

Cucumbers, in particular, had to be fermented at the very end of the season when they no longer needed as much watering, which meant they had a firm texture and their taste was rounder and sweeter, almost like unripe melon. Mum would put them in a jar with water, salt, and tannin-rich leaves picked from shrubs or trees in the garden and, within days, we'd have the tastiest pickles. Then, with the pickling brine, we'd make an excellent winter pork broth – you can find a vegetarian version of it on page 144. Cucumbers aren't the only thing Ukrainians ferment, though. Kherson Steppes, the region I am from, is famous for its watermelons: come August, precarious-looking, stripy pyramids of 50-pound monsters, piled up on trucks by the side of the road, are a familiar sight. Of course, we ferment those as well. Whole apples are also fermented in brine and straw, or even in pumpkin mash.

In the cellar of my house in London, the shelves are slowly getting filled with jars: green tomatoes, chiles, apples, sauerkraut, and all sorts of crazy *kvas* concoctions for when I fancy a refreshing kombucha-like drink or want to perk up a soup. They elate me, they trigger memories, and they inspire me to cook creatively. If they help me to have a healthy gut too, it is only a bonus.

I learned about fermenting from my mum and her mum, who both followed the traditional practices developed in rural Ukraine – but, living in an urban environment, I initially found that sometimes my stuff went moldy or just plain died the next day, even though I was using organic ingredients. Keen to understand why this might be, I discovered that back at home, where my family ferments food on a regular basis, the right bacteria and yeasts are more likely to be present in the air. In cities, however, chemicals and pollutants can inhibit the growth of good bacteria, allowing less desirable ones to sneak into your pickle brine and make it go bad. To try to avoid this, I've adjusted some elements of the traditional recipes given here – and there are also some general guidelines on page 74 to help get your pickling adventures off to a good start.

Quick-fermented cucumbers

MAKES ENOUGH TO FILL
A 3-QT JAR

4 tsp sea salt

10 pink or black peppercorns

5 allspice berries

Handful of horseradish or blackcurrant leaves, or pinch of black tea leaves

2 lb small cucumbers (or large English ones, cut lengthwise into quarters)

1 red chile, thinly sliced

10 garlic cloves, thinly sliced

2 celery ribs, 1 thinly sliced, 1 left whole

1–2 heads of dill flowers or handful of chopped dill stalks

My father loves a barely fermented, fresh pickle. My mum and I prefer them "nuclear" – when they have turned an olive color, and taste fiercely sour and fizzy. You can get your cucumbers to that stage by letting them ferment for a month or two. The leaves are there to add flavor, as well as the tannins that help to keep the cucumbers crunchy.

These simple pickles are incredibly versatile and can be added to soups and stews (such as the mushroom broth on page 144), served alongside the goat stew on page 264 or with cold meats, or just eaten straight from the jar!

Pour 1 quart of water into a saucepan, add the salt, and bring to a simmer, stirring to dissolve the salt. Add the peppercorns and allspice, then switch off the heat and let the brine cool down to room temperature.

Lay the leaves in the base of a sterilized 3-quart jar with a lid, then pack in the cucumbers, chile, garlic, sliced celery, and dill. Pour in the brine, making sure everything is completely covered. If the cucumbers bob up again, wedge the whole celery rib across the neck of the jar to keep them submerged.

Cover with the sterilized lid and leave at room temperature for at least 24 hours. In warm weather, the cucumbers might start to ferment within this time, but if it's cooler, they may take 2 days. When they're ready, the top of the jar will be frothy: use a fork to take out a piece of cucumber to taste – it should be gently and pleasantly sour. If it doesn't taste much different from fresh cucumber, give them another day. If the weather is cool, you may need to allow 3 days anyway.

When you are happy with the result, and you don't want the cucumbers to get much stronger, pop the jar into the fridge to slow down the fermentation process. If you like some funk in your life, leave them for another few days in your kitchen or a cool cellar to keep fermenting.

Sauerkraut with whole cabbage leaves

MAKES ENOUGH TO FILL
A 1-QT CONTAINER

Although there are some really excellent krauts in the shops right now, I'm afraid none of them are quite as good as this one. Apart from anything else, it is worth making your own so you can pickle some whole leaves of cabbage underneath the main kraut. This means that when you get to the bottom of your jar or crock, you can pluck out these leaves, stuff them with some pork belly and rice, and cook them in a white sauce – just like my half-Moldovan grandmother did. Or you can do as they do in Ivano-Frankivsk, in western Ukraine, and stuff the whole kraut leaves with cooked coarse polenta and fried *salo* (cured pork fat).

If you want to line the base of your jar with whole leaves, try to find the softer sweetheart, or pointed, cabbage – the green cabbage generally available is much more robust than Ukrainian varieties, and is rarely sold young, so that even after fermentation the leaves are sometimes too tough to roll. Feel free to add grated apple or quince, or some cranberries, to your sauerkraut for extra interest. Once your sauerkraut is ready, do try the addictive salad of kraut, apple, and celery on page 208.

4¾ lb sweetheart or
young green cabbages

14 oz carrots

About 1½ Tbsp sea salt

Carefully take off the outer leaves of the cabbages and set them aside for later – you should have about 1 lb of whole leaves.

Cut the cabbages in half, cut out the cores, and then cut them into thin matchsticks. (In Ukraine, the core, or heart, of the cabbage is never wasted – it is a prized, sweet morsel and is given to children to be eaten raw. I give it to my son.)

Slice the rest of the cabbage, but not too thinly. You should have about 2¾ lb of shredded cabbage, making 1½ tablespoons of salt pretty much perfect. If you have less shredded cabbage than this, reduce the salt accordingly; if more, increase it slightly.

Scrub or peel your carrots (if they are clean, I rarely peel them), then cut a little lengthwise slice off each carrot to make it steady on your chopping board. Cut the carrots lengthwise into thin slices and then into thin matchsticks – or you could just grate them on the coarse side of a box grater.

Mix half the shredded cabbage and half the carrots in a large bowl and add half the salt. My mother just massages it all with her hands (she is fitter than me, despite being 62!), but after massaging it for a bit, I usually reach for my granite pestle and pummel the cabbage until it is defeated, soft and succulent. Then repeat the operation with the rest of the cabbage, carrots, and salt.

Put a little bit of the shredded cabbage in the base of a sterilized 1½-quart container with a lid, then lay in your whole cabbage leaves – if they are too awkward and concave, just slice them in half. Pile in the rest of the cabbage.

Now you need to weigh down the kraut so it releases enough liquid to cover everything – I usually put a sturdy small plate on top of the cabbage and sit my heavy granite pestle on top of that, then wait until a layer of brine forms on the surface. At this point, cover the container with its sterilized lid and leave at room temperature for a couple of days, lifting the lid from time to time to release the fermentation gases.

When the kraut tastes sour, transfer it to a colder place, where it should keep well for about 3 months – a cellar is perfect, but a fridge, or in winter in cold climates a garden shed or outside on your balcony would be fine too.

Fermented Gagauz stuffed peppers

MAKES ENOUGH TO FILL
A 5-QT CROCK OR WIDE-
MOUTHED JAR

2–3 tsp superfine sugar
(golden, if available)

2 bay leaves

1 tsp black peppercorns

2½ Tbsp sea salt

Small handful dill stalks and
flower heads

¼ cup finely diced celery

10 garlic cloves, thinly sliced

1 lb green cabbage,
thinly sliced

1 Tbsp vegetable oil

1½ cups sliced onion

2 carrots, coarsely grated

2 Tbsp tomato paste

1 red or green chile, sliced

2½ lb red or yellow peppers
(about 4 large or 6 medium)

½ lb cherry tomatoes

If you try only one pickle recipe in this book, please make it this one, known as *turshu* (meaning "sour"). The Gagauz are a Christian Turkic people who live in the southwest of Ukraine and Moldova – and, in my humble opinion, they make some of the most delicious fermented pickles in the world. Stuffed with cabbage and chiles, these sweet and sour peppers are "moreish" and nutritious. And it is not just tomatoes you can drop into the brine along with the cabbage-stuffed peppers: you could also add small cucumbers, cauliflower florets, sliced carrots, or green beans.

Pour 2 quarts of water into a large pan and add the sugar, bay leaves, peppercorns, and 2 tablespoons of the salt. Bring to a boil and stir well to dissolve the salt and sugar – as soon as they have dissolved, switch the heat off. Add the dill, celery, and garlic, then leave the brine to cool until it is just warm.

Meanwhile, in a large bowl, mix the cabbage with the remaining ½ tablespoon of salt and massage it until it is soft and has released its juices. (My mother just uses her hands to massage the cabbage, but I make use of a heavy granite pestle to gently pummel the cabbage first, before getting my hands in there.)

Heat the oil in a frying pan over medium-low heat. Add the onion and cook for a couple of minutes until it softens, then add the carrots and keep cooking until the onion is just starting to turn golden. Add the tomato paste and cook for a minute, then add the chile and cook for another minute. Leave to cool before mixing into the massaged cabbage.

Cut the tops off the peppers and carefully hollow out the pith and seeds. Stuff the peppers with the cabbage, using your hands to pack it in tightly. Place the peppers into a sterilized 5-quart crock or jar, standing them upright and nestling them side by side, in two layers if need be. Pour in the warm brine, then add the whole tomatoes. Make sure everything is submerged before covering the jar or crock and leaving it in a cool, dark place for 2 days. If it's late summertime – which it should be when peppers are plentiful enough to make this! – the brine should start bubbling and the ferment will start to smell mouthwateringly good in a day or so.

After 2 days, scoop out a little bit of cabbage and taste it: if it tastes like kraut, it is time to put it somewhere a little colder for the next couple of days, but not in the fridge just yet.

When the stuffed peppers have fermented enough for you, store in the fridge and eat alongside grilled meat or anything else that would be complemented by a sweet, sour, and spicy pickle.

Fermented chiles

---

4 tsp sea salt

20 red or green chiles

½ lb celery and/or lovage leaves, washed

1 celery rib, if needed

This is one of the easiest and most satisfying ferments to make. Traditionally, long red chiles are used, but if you can get hold of them, fruity habaneros are fantastic. You can add whatever flavorings you like: lovage or celery leaves work well, as do sliced garlic cloves and the stronger-tasting soft herbs, such as tarragon.

When the chiles are ready, the skins will be quite tough to eat, so I like to squeeze out the beautifully soft and fizzy flesh and blitz it into a paste in the blender. It is then excellent used as a condiment, or to spike up a rich winter borsch, split pea soup, or some spelt dumplings (page 172); this summer, my husband mixed a spoonful with some yogurt to dress a slaw. Do play around and get creative with it: think relishes and salsas, curries and stews, marinades for grilled meat, fish, and vegetables – the possibilities really are endless.

Pour 1 quart of water into a saucepan, add the salt, and bring to a boil, stirring to dissolve the salt. Switch off the heat, then leave the brine to cool down to room temperature.

Put the chiles and leaves into a sterilized 2-quart jar with a lid, then pour in the brine, making sure everything is completely covered. If the chiles bob up again, wedge a spare celery rib across the neck of the jar to keep them submerged.

Cover with the sterilized lid and leave at room temperature for a few days, lifting the lid from time to time to release any fermentation gases. When you notice the brine becoming playfully fizzy, transfer the ferment to the fridge, where it will keep for many months, slowly getting more intensely sour and spicy.

Fermented tomato pulp

MAKES ENOUGH TO FILL
A 1-QT JAR

---

2 lb ripe tomatoes

4 tsp sea salt

Called *mors* in Ukraine, this is a good way to preserve tomatoes if you have an excess of ripe, juicy fruit: the pulp goes sour, fizzy, and irresistible. It will last in the fridge for up to a month. If you want to keep it for longer, do as they do in Ukraine and stop the fermentation process by boiling the jar of tomato pulp in a saucepan of water for about 10 minutes, then seal and store in a cool, dark place – it should last through the winter and beyond.

Chop the tomatoes and mix them, along with any juices that have escaped onto the chopping board, with the salt. Put into a sterilized 1-quart jar and cover with the lid – the tomatoes should release enough juices to completely cover. Leave in a dark place at room temperature until they start bubbling and taste sour and slightly fizzy. This should take about 2–3 days if it's warm, longer in cooler weather – do not worry if a layer of white yeast forms on top, as long as the ferment smells fine (you can either scrape it off and discard it, or just leave it be).

Transfer the tomatoes to a food processor and blitz to a pulp, then return to the jar. Store the fermented tomato pulp in the fridge, where it will keep for up to a month. Use it to add a sour note to borsch, as the base for a tomato sauce when cooking fish, or as the basis for a very good Bloody Mary.

Apples fermented in pumpkin mash

MAKES ENOUGH TO FILL
A 2-QT JAR

1¾ lb Golden Delicious
or Goldrush apples

2 lb baking pumpkin or
hard-shelled squash, peeled

About 2 Tbsp sea salt

This is an old recipe that was given to me by Asya Oleksiyivna Berezko, my perfumer friend Victoria Frolova's great-grandmother; her own mother used to make it every autumn. Asya used a sweet pumpkin, and as for the apples, she told me Calville was the best variety. Calville can be hard to find, but I've had good luck with Golden Delicious and Goldrush (try the suppliers on pages 340–1): they should be neither too ripe nor too green.

When the fermented apples are ready, they should be sour but still firm, with a beautiful amber-golden color and a perfume of red berries, which permeates the pumpkin. It will take about three months to reach this point, but the wait is well worth it.

Make sure the apples you have are as perfect as possible, with no bruises or blemishes. Remove any stems.

Cut the pumpkin into chunks and put into a saucepan with 1 quart of water. Bring to a boil, then simmer over medium-low heat until it is very soft and some of the water has evaporated. Mash the pumpkin, along with its cooking liquid. Weigh how much pumpkin mash you have, then stir in 2.5 percent of its weight in salt, or about 1 tablespoon salt per pound. So, if you have 2 pounds of mash, add 2 tablespoons of salt. Let the mash cool down until it is just warm.

Pack the apples into a sterilized 2-quart jar with a lid, then pour over the warm mash, making sure the apples are completely covered. (If they are not, make a brine using ½ tsp salt for every ½ cup of water, stir well, and use to top up the jar.) Close the lid and leave in a warm place for 2–3 months, depending on the temperature. Open the lid from time to time to check on it – the ferment should smell pleasantly sour.

If you are doing this in late summer or early autumn, check the apples after 2 weeks. Take one out and slice a little bit off to taste: its flesh should still be white, and it should taste fizzy and sour. If you are doing this in the colder months, the fermentation will likely take at least 2 months. It should not bubble up aggressively, the pumpkin mash will only release an occasional, slow pop. When the apples and pumpkin have fermented enough for you, store in the fridge or cellar.

The fermented apples are good in a salad, such as the one with celery and sauerkraut on page 208, and the pumpkin mash is delicious served as a sauce for cauliflower fritters (page 192). If most of the apples are firm but the bottom ones have gone to mush, do not worry – just blitz the mushed ones in a food processor with the pumpkin, season with some more salt, and pepper if needed and serve as an accompaniment to pork.

Pickled watermelon

MAKES ENOUGH TO FILL
A 3-QT JAR

---

2 Tbsp runny honey

1 Tbsp sea salt

½ cup raw cider vinegar

1 tsp allspice berries

4½ lb watermelon

Have you ever seen a field of watermelons? It is quite eerie, almost post-apocalyptic – a thousand green beach balls abandoned. Faced with such an expanse of ripe watermelons, Ukrainians pickle them, using raw cider vinegar to initiate the process.

Pickled watermelon is excellent as an accompaniment to fatty meats, or it can be sliced into salads or eaten as a vodka chaser. And some of the watermelon flesh, blitzed with a little of the brine and sieved, would make a wonderful base for a winter cocktail.

In a saucepan, mix 6 cups of water with the honey, salt, vinegar, and allspice berries. Bring the brine to a simmer, then switch off the heat and leave to cool down until it's just warm.

Meanwhile, cut the watermelon into small triangular slices, cutting away all of the dark green outer layer, but keeping the pale-green pith beneath.

Put your watermelon slices into a sterilized 3-quart jar with a lid, then pour in the warm brine and close the lid tightly. Turn the jar upside down and leave at room temperature for a couple of days, then move it to the cellar or fridge.

Fermented watermelons

MAKES ENOUGH TO FILL
A 2½-GAL CONTAINER

As you may have figured out by now, Ukrainians will ferment anything, and watermelons are no exception. When she was growing up, my mum remembers a defunct old bathtub that lived in a shady part of the garden, where my grandfather would ferment vast quantities of watermelon. For posterity, here is a recipe for whole fermented watermelons, though I'll admit it might be a bit ambitious for most of us – unless, of course, you happen to have an old bathtub in your back garden.

This requires a 2½-gallon container: traditionally oak barrels (or bathtubs!) were used, but nowadays it tends to be made in large stockpots or plastic containers. The leaves infuse the brine with tannins that help to keep the watermelon crisp. You can also use the juice of the watermelons instead of water in the brine. Feel free to add other flavorings to the brine: celery, allspice, and garlic are common; I imagine ginger would work very well too.

10 Tbsp (150g) sea salt
(or 1 cup/250g if using
watermelon juice for the brine)

5 watermelons, about 6 inches
in diameter (plus an extra
10 or so for juicing if you want
to ferment the melons in juice)

½ cup (50g) organic whole-
grain rye flour – optional

2 branches of sour cherry,
blackcurrant, or oak,
leaves picked

If using water for the brine, heat up 1 cup of water and dissolve the 10 tablespoons salt in this, then stir it into 5 quarts of fresh water.

If you want to use watermelon juice for the brine, juice enough watermelons to give you 5 quarts of juice – the simplest way to do this is to push the flesh through a sieve to catch the seeds, collecting the juice in a large bowl beneath. Mix 1 cup of salt into the juice, stirring it vigorously to help the salt dissolve.

If you like, you can add the rye flour to the brine to help speed up the fermentation process, mixing it in well. Pierce the watermelons all over with a metal skewer – this will also encourage them to ferment faster.

Make sure your clean 2½-gallon container is in a cool, dark place, ideally a cellar, before you fill it, as it will be difficult to move once it is full. Lay the leaves in the base, then pack in the whole watermelons. Pour the brine over, filling it to the brim, then cover with a clean piece of cloth or cheesecloth and put the lid on top to keep the watermelons submerged in the brine.

Fermentation will take at least 40 days, or even longer – it will all depend on the surrounding temperature. Check the cloth or cheesecloth and the lid from time to time, and rinse them with boiling water if any white yeast forms on them. Forty days is rather a long haul, admittedly, but it is worth it – pretty much the whole watermelon can be consumed, even the dark green outer layer.

Fermented damsons from Opishnya

MAKES ENOUGH TO FILL A
4-QT JAR OR CONTAINER

In Poltava, in central Ukraine, a lot of the recipes I encountered for preserving plums used sugar and vinegar to pickle them, and they were very delicious. However, I also kept hearing about the famous "salted" (i.e. fermented) plums from Opishnya. Dating back to the seventeenth century, these wondrous plums would be wheeled around local markets and were served on platters to tsars, so good were they. They are mentioned in Ivan Kotliarevsky's poem *Eneida*, written in 1798, and also in *Pan Khalyavskiy*, a novel by Hryhory Kvitka. Writing in 1839, Kvitka describes a lavish feast that includes "…chickens 50, ducks 20, geese likewise, suckling pigs 10. A hog would inevitably have been slaughtered, as well as a couple of rams and one whole cow… As soon as one type of borsch was finished, another one would follow. Borsch with beef; borsch with a fatty goose; pork borsch; Sobievsky borsch, Skoropadskiy borsch… The soups, again of all different sorts, were put on another table; a noodle soup, a soup with rice and raisins and many others… The third table carried dishes that were called "sweet." Those included ducks with raisins and prunes with a red sauce, beef shank with almonds; brains, and various sweet root vegetables, turnips, carrots and others, everything delicious… The fourth table was made up of different roasted birds, suckling pigs, hares, etc., salted gherkins, dressed with vinegar and garlic and the famous Opishnya plums…"

Here is the recipe, using damsons. These are great with fatty meats, such as roast duck, pork, or lamb, or roast pumpkin – but feel free to serve them with Kvitka's outlandish menu suggestions!

4½ lb firm organic damsons
(or any fleshy rather than
juicy plums)

2 Tbsp sea salt

4 Tbsp raw honey

3 bay leaves

1 Tbsp allspice berries

2 Tbsp organic whole-grain
rye flour
or
1 Tbsp rye starter (page 150)

Organic straw
(rye, if you can find it)

Before you get started, please note that this is an old recipe, and it dates from a time when most people lived in the countryside, fermented a lot, and regularly made sourdough bread. If this doesn't sound like the way you live, I suggest you test half the amount of damsons and brine first, without the straw. Assuming your damsons are organic, I wouldn't wash them, as the natural yeasts clinging to their skins will help the fermentation process. Follow the recipe below, putting the damsons into a sterilized 1.5-quart jar with a lid, and making sure they are fully submerged in the brine. Cover with the lid and keep them somewhere fairly cool and dark for 5 days, lifting the lid from time to time to release any fermentation gases. Transfer to the fridge and let them finish fermenting for a week or so.

When you're ready to try the full amount with straw, boil 1½ quarts of water in your kettle, then leave to cool slightly. Put the salt into a large heatproof bowl and pour in the hot water from the kettle,

stirring to dissolve the salt fully. When the brine is no longer hot, but is still warm, add the honey, bay leaves, allspice berries, and the rye flour or starter, stirring well.

Traditionally, wooden barrels are used for this ferment, but a 1-gallon container or jar with a lid works well. Put a layer of straw in the base, add the damsons, and cover with more straw. Lay some cheesecloth over the top, then weigh down with something heavy to keep the damsons submerged (I use a sturdy plate with an old granite pestle on it), then pour in the brine, making sure the damsons and the straw are both covered with brine. Now cover with the lid. Leave somewhere dark – and, given that damson season is late summer or early autumn, fairly cool – for a couple of weeks. Do check on them every so often: if some white yeast forms, don't worry, just take the top layer of straw out and throw it away, then carefully lift the white yeast off the brine and wash the cheesecloth. Put some fresh straw on top and then the clean cloth.

The damsons are ready when they become paler and softer – they should taste sweet, sour, and slightly fizzy. Once this happens, transfer to a colder place, such as a cellar, garden shed, or balcony, where they should keep well for up to 3 months. The brine will be pink and delicious to drink (it makes a great hangover cure!).

Fermented physalis

MAKES ENOUGH TO FILL
A 1.5-QT JAR

---

4 tsp sea salt

1 lb physalis (or tomatillos or
small green tomatoes), papery
skins removed

A few horseradish leaves –
optional

1 red or green chile, thinly sliced

6 garlic cloves, thinly sliced

Although they might occasionally find their way onto somebody's birthday cake as a decoration, we never really cooked with physalis when I was growing up.

However, many years later, when I visited the Danylchenko family in a summer kitchen near Kyiv, they served us pickled, or rather fermented, physalis. And it turns out that their texture is perfect for fermentation, and they taste like pickled green tomatoes. Serve them as a pickle alongside other dishes.

If you have a glut of physalis (or their cousin, tomatillos), they are also good dried in a very low oven overnight until they're like raisins, and then used in a rice pilaf.

Boil 1 quart of water in your kettle, then leave to cool down slightly. Put the salt into a large heatproof bowl and pour in the hot water from the kettle, stirring to dissolve the salt fully.

Put the physalis in a colander in the sink and boil a fresh kettle, then pour hot water over the physalis – this helps to lift the natural sticky, oily film from their skin.

Put the physalis and all the remaining ingredients into a sterilized 1.5-quart jar with a lid, then pour in the brine. Close the lid and leave at room temperature for a week, or until the brine tastes sour and fizzy, lifting the lid from time to time to release any fermentation gases. Transfer to a colder place, such as a cellar or the fridge, where the physalis will keep well for up to 3 months.

Sour eggplant with mint and chile

MAKES ENOUGH TO FILL
A 3-QT GLASS OR PLASTIC
CONTAINER

10 young slender eggplants

1 whole garlic bulb, cloves
separated and peeled

2-4 chiles, stems removed

Picked leaves from 1 bunch
mint

Picked leaves from 1 bunch
flat-leaf parsley

2½ Tbsp sea salt

1-2 Tbsp superfine sugar
(golden, if available)

My Ukrainian friend Katrya Kalyuzhna, who lives in the same town where I grew up, showed me her mum's old handwritten recipe book, which had a vinegar-pickled eggplant and mint recipe. We tried making it, and it was delicious – but Katrya, who finds a certain joy in fermenting things in brine, decided to adapt the original recipe and came up with this: a pickle to surprise and inspire. I urge you to give it a go. My British husband loves these eggplants breaded and fried, then served with sour cream, but I think that's a bit of a perversion! I just eat them as a pickle, part of a hearty winter meal.

Cook the whole eggplants in a large saucepan of boiling water for 20 minutes, until tender, then drain and leave to cool. Lay the eggplants in a deep baking dish and sit a chopping board directly on them. Place a heavy object on top, to really press them down, then leave overnight at room temperature, to extract as much liquid as possible.

Next day, to make the stuffing for the eggplants, finely chop the garlic, chiles, mint, and parsley together (or blitz them in a food processor).

Boil 1 quart of water in your kettle. Put the salt and sugar into a large heatproof bowl and pour in the hot water from the kettle, stirring to dissolve completely. Leave the brine to cool.

Cut each eggplant in half lengthwise, stopping just short of the stalk end, so the two halves are still attached. Open out and stuff some of the green paste inside, then press the two halves back together and place in a sterilized 3-quart rectangular glass or plastic container. Repeat with the rest of the eggplants and stuffing.

Pour the brine over the eggplants. Cover with a lid and leave at room temperature for 3 days – or longer if it's cold. Once the eggplants taste sour, put them into a cellar or the fridge, where they will keep for up to 3 months, maturing and getting better all the time.

Pickled cabbage leaves with beet

MAKES ENOUGH TO FILL
A 2-QUART JAR

4 tsp sea salt

½ cup superfine sugar (golden,
if available)

½ cup raw cider vinegar

1 small green cabbage

1¾ oz horseradish root, peeled
and sliced

½ lb beets, peeled and
cut into thin wedges

The Besarabsky food market in Kyiv is spectacular, if expensive by local standards. It has an impressive pickle section, where I first saw *pelyustka* – cabbage leaves pickled with beet to look like pink rose petals. The market versions were tasty, but this recipe (kindly given to me by another Olga) comes from Nyzhne Selyshche, a village in Transcarpathia where they make the most delicious pickles. The addition of vinegar means that the cabbage keeps for much longer and remains crunchy. It is fantastic eaten as it is, like a pickled salad of sorts, or as part of a bigger feast.

Boil just under 1 quart of water in your kettle. Put the salt and sugar into a large heatproof bowl and pour in the hot water from the kettle, stirring to dissolve completely. Stir in the vinegar.

Meanwhile, core the cabbage (don't throw the core away: you can chop it up and use it in this recipe, or just eat it as a snack), then cut the cabbage in half and then into 4-inch squares – these will be your "petals." Put the horseradish in the base of a sterilized 2-quart jar with a lid. Now add a third of the beets, then a third of the cabbage, and keep alternating these two layers until all the beet and cabbage is used up.

Pour over the hot brine, let it cool to room temperature, and then close the lid. Leave somewhere warm and dark for 1–2 weeks, depending on the temperature. When it becomes fizzy, move it somewhere cooler: a cellar is ideal, but the fridge will do.

This pickle will keep for ages – long enough to last you through the winter, for sure – and will stay sweet, sour, and crunchy.

Sour cherry and garlic condiment

MAKES ENOUGH TO FILL
A 1-QT JAR

In the UK, I have spent sixteen long years desperately looking for sour cherries. In my hometown in Ukraine they are everywhere, dropping on your head and staining your sandaled feet as you walk down the street. During their short season, they will be frozen, made into jams, and preserved whole (with pits) in sugared water to make a cherry liqueur for drinking over winter.

This recipe is a Ukrainian adaptation of the Georgian *tkemali* – a sour plum purée spiked with garlic and chile. Why let all those cherries go to waste, splattered on your head, when you can pick them and turn them into something so delicious? In the absence of sour cherries, you can make it with regular cherries, raspberries, blackberries, or blackcurrants. This condiment is delicious whisked into a dressing for baked or boiled beets or served with poultry.

2 lb sour cherries, pitted

¾ cup superfine sugar (golden, if available)

4 tsp sea salt

5-6 garlic cloves, finely chopped

1 chile, finely chopped

Put the cherries in a heavy-based saucepan, cover, and let them simmer for 15 minutes. Using a hand blender, blitz the cherries thoroughly, then add the sugar, salt, garlic, and chile and briefly blitz again to combine. Cook for another 15 minutes.

Taste the sauce: it should be perfectly sweet, sour, salty, and spicy. If not, adjust with more sugar or salt. Transfer to a sterilized 1-quart lidded jar and keep in the fridge.

Zucchini "caviar"

MAKES ENOUGH TO FILL
A 1.2-QT JAR

My first real food memory is of zucchini caviar, very smooth and mustard-yellow – it was the one thing I enjoyed at kindergarten. I only went for a few months, when I was four, but the whole experience was so traumatic that my memories are very clear. The kindergarten, called *Ryabinushka* ("Little Rowan Berry"), felt bleak and sterile, like a hospital; the murals were terrifying, and it smelled funny.

Then, for lunch, there would be shop-bought zucchini paste. We never had shop-bought preserves at home – with homemade versions, there was never any need to – but whatever its provenance, that zucchini caviar brought me momentary comfort. Here is the superior homemade version. Spread it over dark rye bread, use as a pasta sauce, or serve with grilled meat.

4½ lb zucchini (or yellow summer squash)

½ cup good-quality sunflower or mild olive oil

1 lb onions, thinly sliced

10 oz carrots, scrubbed and coarsely grated

¼ cup tomato paste

1¾ lb ripe, flavorsome fresh tomatoes
or
2 x 14.5-oz cans of diced tomatoes

5 big garlic cloves, crushed

Sea salt and black pepper

Cut the zucchini in half lengthwise, then thinly slice them crosswise into half-moons (or put the halved zucchini through a food processor with a slicing attachment).

Heat ¼ cup of the oil in a large saucepan over medium-low heat. Add the onions and cook until they start to soften and color. If the pan looks dry, add a splash of water and scrape the base with a wooden spoon. Add the carrots and tomato paste and cook, stirring from time to time, until the carrots also soften, then cook for another 5–10 minutes. Now add the zucchini, turn the heat up to medium, and cook for 10 minutes, stirring regularly. When they start to collapse, reduce the heat to low and cook gently for 30 minutes, stirring regularly. You want the zucchini to keep catching on the pan slightly so they caramelize, but be sure to scrape the pan with your spoon from time to time, adding splashes of water to stop them from burning.

If using fresh tomatoes, grate on the coarse side of a box grater, discarding the skins. Add the tomatoes and garlic to the pan, increase the heat to medium-high, and cook for 30–40 minutes, stirring regularly – you can help things along by gently crushing the vegetables with a masher. Season to taste: I like just salt and pepper, but feel free to add a little spice. When the zucchini mixture starts spitting fervently, lower the heat and keep cooking until you end up with a thick, brown paste. When it's ready, it should have reduced to about 1 quart, but do check in a measuring jug before putting it into the jar, just in case.

Transfer your hot zucchini caviar to a sterilized 1-quart jar with a lid. To help it keep for longer, pour the remaining oil over the top to seal and make sure the zucchini caviar is completely covered with a layer of oil at all times. Cover with the lid and let it cool before storing in the fridge or a cellar for up to 2 months.

Pickled mushrooms

MAKES ENOUGH TO FILL
A 1-QT JAR

¾ cup raw cider vinegar

1 heaping tsp sea salt

¼ cup soft brown sugar

1 bay leaf, torn

½ tsp allspice berries

4 garlic cloves, thinly sliced

1 red chile, bruised – optional

10 oz fresh shiitake or button
mushrooms

Unrefined sunflower oil
(or pumpkin seed or walnut
oil), and thinly sliced onion,
to serve

In Ukraine and throughout Eastern Europe, many people ferment mushrooms, but personally I find them a little too slimy and weird that way. I much prefer a vinegar-pickled mushroom. The addition of chile is not at all traditional, but I enjoy spice. Do play around with the flavorings. These are extremely "moreish" and you will finish the jar quickly – but the good news is that you can then re-use the pickling liquor to make another batch.

To make the pickling liquor, pour ¾ cup of water into a medium saucepan, then stir in the vinegar, salt and sugar, bay leaf, allspice, garlic and chile, if using. Give it a quick taste and adjust the balance of acid (vinegar), salt, and sugar to suit your palate.

Add the mushrooms to the pickling liquor and bring to a boil, keeping an eye on it as it tends to boil over easily. Turn down to a simmer and cook for about 10 minutes, then switch off the heat and leave to cool.

Transfer the mushrooms and their pickling liquor to a 1-quart jar with a lid. Close the lid and store in the fridge for up to 3 months.

Serve the pickled mushrooms with a little nutty oil and some thinly sliced onion.

Pork preserved for winter

MAKES ENOUGH TO FILL
3 X 16-OZ JARS
(OR 1 X 50-OZ JAR)

When I asked my mother to help me test this retro dish in my kitchen in London, we scoffed half a jar in two days, heaped onto rye bread. She promptly declared that she was going to make a batch on her return home, explaining that my dad would like it – and having a jar of this in the fridge would discourage him from buying rubbish processed sausages!

Historically, pigs were slaughtered for winter, but only the offal would be eaten fresh. The rest of the animal would be butchered and preserved over the course of a long and arduous day. Some of the cuts of pork with a good amount of fat on them would be packed into clay pots with a splash of water and placed in the wood-fired oven at the end of the day, when the heat would naturally be fading. The meat would slowly cook until it was tender enough to be scooped up with a spoon, and if there weren't enough natural juices and fat to cover the meat, some lard would be poured into the pots. They were then left to cool, covered with some clean cotton cloth (to allow the preserve "to breathe") and kept in the cellar until spring. This same method of preservation is still used today, except that now the meat is cooked and kept in tubby glass jars.

---

2 lb fatty pork shoulder or leg

2 tsp sea salt

2 onions, finely diced

10 black peppercorns

6 allspice berries

2 bay leaves

About 14 Tbsp good-quality lard, to seal, if needed

Cut the pork into 1½-inch chunks, leaving all the fat on. Mix with the salt, onions, spices, and ¼ cup of water, then pack into three 16-oz jars with lids, leaving a ½-inch space between the meat and the neck of the jar. Sit the jars on a baking sheet or roasting pan and cover with foil. Put into a cold oven, then switch it on to 300°F. Leave the jars of pork to cook for about 3–4 hours, or until the meat is falling apart, then mush it up with a fork into a coarse pâté, not unlike French *pâté de campagne.*

If there isn't enough natural pork fat and juices in the jar to cover the meat completely, melt some lard and carefully pour into the jars. Put on the sterilized lids, making sure they're on tight, and turn the jars upside down while they cool.

Turn the jars the right way up, remove the lids, and put a circle of waxed paper on top of the pork, then replace the lids. Store somewhere cool, like a cellar or the fridge, where the pork will keep for months.

When you take some of it out, make sure the remaining meat is completely covered in lard with no bits poking out, and there are no air pockets in the jar.

Chile paste

MAKES ENOUGH TO FILL
A 10-OZ JAR

Do you ever buy a big bag of chiles, only to watch them wither before you've had chance to use them all? Well, this is the best way to save them – made into this versatile paste, which is almost like a wet chile salt, they will keep for a long time. Similar chile pastes can easily be bought in shops in Ukraine and Hungary, but this is so easy to make and so good to have in the fridge. In the summer, you could throw the chiles on the barbecue first until they blister a little, to add extra flavor.

Add a spoonful of this chile paste to a meaty stew, such as *bogracz* (page 260), broths or marinades, even curries; it's also outstanding smeared over the sour cabbage rolls on page 258.

12 red chiles (9 oz)

4 tsp sea salt

¼ cup good-quality wine vinegar or cider vinegar

¼ cup extra-virgin olive oil

Cut the chiles in half lengthwise and take out the seeds, or leave them in if you enjoy your food hot.

In a blender or food processor, blitz the chiles to a fine paste with the salt, vinegar, and oil, then pour into a sterilized 10-ounce jar with a lid. Put on the lid and store in the fridge, where it will keep for a few months.

Use sparingly, as it is quite salty – the salt content is what makes it last so well.

Salted herbs for winter

MAKES ENOUGH TO FILL
A 12-OZ JAR

8 oz herbs and greens, such as dill, parsley, green onions, sorrel, and wild garlic, washed

1½ Tbsp sea salt

Cooking without herbs would be considered unfathomable in Ukraine. Yet only a few generations ago, fresh herbs were unavailable during the cold months. And so, every summer, my grandmother would preserve fresh herbs in salt: although they lost their vibrant color and became mildly fermented in the process, they were delicious. Known as a "green borsch mix for winter," these salted herbs would most often be used as a base for the soup of greens that is normally cooked in spring (page 128). My grandmother would also add the rinsed herbs to other soups and stews.

Of course you can buy herbs all year around now, but the flavor of this particular preserve is so interesting that I still make it, especially when I have an abundance of herbs in my garden.

I use the stalks as well as the leaves here, so nothing goes to waste. (In fact, you can just use stalks, so if you end up with lots of leftover stalks from other recipes, save them for salting.)

Finely chop all the herbs and mix them together. Put a layer of herbs in the base of a sterilized 12-ounce jar with a lid and sprinkle over some of the salt. Now add another layer of herbs and more salt, pressing the herbs down with your hand. Keep alternating these layers until you run out of herbs and salt, packing them in tightly as you go.

Cover with a lid and leave at room temperature for 2–3 days (you might want to push the herbs down a little further on the second day). Once a layer of liquid has formed at the top, move the jar to the cellar or fridge, where the salted herbs will keep for several months.

The herbs will be quite salty, so use them in small amounts as a seasoning or give them a quick rinse first.

Beet and horseradish

MAKES ENOUGH TO FILL
AN 8-OZ JAR

This Christmas and Easter treat, called *tsvikli* in western Ukraine, came into Ukrainian cuisine from Ashkenazi Jews – whose name for the dish is *chrain*.

Ukrainians often put more horseradish than beet into their *tsvikli*, so it is barely pink, rather than the deep purplish-red color of beet – but, much as I love the fiery heat of horseradish, I prefer the smooth velvetiness and bright color that comes from using more beet. If you want to reverse the quantities, do 1½ ounces of beet to 14 ounces of horseradish – this really should be called *chrain* (meaning horseradish), rather than *tsvikli* (meaning beet) – and then use it very sparingly, like mustard. If you can get hold of raspberry or blackcurrant vinegar, do try it here; berry vinegars go really well with beet.

Traditionally this is served as a condiment alongside the Christmas feast, with poached chicken or cold roast meat, or even with pork set in aspic. For a more modern rendition, spread a little on toast and top with soft goat cheese and fresh cherries.

14 oz beets

1½ oz horseradish root, peeled

1 Tbsp sea salt

1 Tbsp honey

¼ cup fruit vinegar, such as raspberry or blackcurrant

Put the whole unpeeled beets into a saucepan and cover with cold water, then bring to a boil and cook for 40 minutes–1 hour, just until they can be easily pierced with a knife. Rinse in cold water, then rub off the skins with your hands and grate the beet on the fine side of a box grater.

Now the hard part: the pain of horseradish. If you have a food processor, do yourself a favor and blitz it in that. Because I am too lazy to clean my processor, I usually just bite the bullet and grate it finely on the box grater. Maybe I secretly enjoy the tears – very Ukrainian of me!

Whisk the salt and honey into the vinegar to dissolve. Add the beet and horseradish, wiping away your tears, then mix very well and give it a taste. It will taste very strong at first, but horseradish tends to dissipate very quickly, so do add more horseradish if you like it strong. Feel free to adjust the seasoning too – adding more salt will make it last longer. If not using right away, transfer the paste to a clean 8-ounce jar. It will keep in the fridge for up to a month.

Dried smoked pears

MAKES 2 LB

4½ lb Bartlett pears, cut in half lengthwise, cores and stems removed

Traditionally, at the end of the day, these pears would be placed, either whole or halved, in the *pich* (wood-fired masonry oven), where they would simultaneously dry and smoke as the oven's heat slowly faded. This would be done with the same batch of pears over the course of a few days, until they were deep and dark, imbued with the scent of cherry wood, and with beautiful grooves in their skin. I may not have a *pich* or a smoker in England, but I am very lucky to know Melissa Rigby and her husband, Chris Wills – who, with a glut of homegrown pears, a Rayburn stove, and a smoker, developed the method given here.

These pears are usually added to borsch (page 132) or *uzvar* (page 314). They are very intensely flavored: just a half a pear is enough to impart a sweet smokiness to pork, duck, pheasant, or lamb stews.

Lay the pears, cut side up, on baking sheets lined with baking parchment and put them in a very low oven – the warming oven of a Rayburn or Aga is ideal – until they are completely dried, about 3 days. Check on them every so often, swapping the sheets around so the pears dry evenly. As they dry, the pears will shrivel and develop a caramelized chewiness – any juice that oozes onto the baking parchment will taste like pear caramel.

Transfer the dried pears to wire racks, placing them cut side up. If you have a cold-smoker, you can then cold-smoke the pears for 18 hours. Alternatively, you can hot-smoke the pears over oak or fruit wood chips on a barbecue for about an hour or so.

Store the pears in lidded glass jars at room temperature – they will last for many months.

Fermented baked milk

MAKES ABOUT 3¾ CUPS

As in many other cultures, Ukrainians have a penchant for calling our children after a relative. We go a little extreme with it sometimes: I have the same name as my mother – we are both Olgas (*big Olga* and *little Olia*, but still) – and my father would not have it any other way. I called my son Sasha after my brother. But my friend Katrya's grandfather Ivan took it to the next level, paying a hundred roubles to her hesitant young parents to call their daughter Kateryna (Katrya), after his wife, whom he loved for her beauty and, most importantly, for her integrity. He did well, as both qualities were definitely passed on to Katrya.

Ryazhanka is the Ukrainian name for this yogurt made from slow-baked milk, and Kateryna the grandmother used to make it almost every night. It is an ancient, delicious way to preserve milk, which is first baked and then left to ferment overnight. To keep the clay pots of milk at the right temperature for fermentation, Kateryna would wrap them in Ivan's old sheepskin coat. In the morning they all enjoyed the freshest and most delicious breakfast: a cup of *ryazhanka* the color of gentlest dawn-pink, and a slice of warm, crusty bread with some apricot jam.

1 quart organic raw or unhomogenized milk

6 Tbsp organic yogurt, at room temperature

Preheat the oven to 225°F.

Pour the milk into an ovenproof pan and bring to a boil, turning off the heat as soon as it starts bubbling. Watch it like a hawk; milk tends to run away easily. Transfer to the oven and bake, uncovered, in the oven overnight – the milk will develop a dark crust. Remove it from the oven and leave to cool to 105°F.

Carefully take off the crust and thoroughly whisk the yogurt into the warm milk, then gently lay the crust back on the surface of the milk. Cover the pan with a lid and place it inside an insulated bag or cover it with a thick blanket (or an old sheepskin coat) and leave it in a warm place overnight.

As the milk thickens, it will develop a slightly sour, caramelly flavor. Once you give it a good stir with a handheld whisk, this is delicious in every way that a really good drinking yogurt should be – and it will keep for up to 5 days in the fridge. (This might be a bit "cheffy," but the crust can also be sprinkled with confectioners' sugar and dehydrated in a low oven to make a tasty crisp!)

Watermelon molasses

MAKES ENOUGH TO FILL
A 16-OZ JAR

After World War II, sugar was very expensive in Ukraine, but watermelons grew in abundance, ready to be preserved in one way or another come September. For watermelon molasses, huge cauldrons holding up to 10 gallons of watermelon juice would be set over a wood fire in the courtyard and slowly stirred for hours. No sugar was added – none was needed as watermelons are already so sweet. What you ended up with was a viscous honey-like paste that smells and tastes like…pumpkin! To be honest, it really was quite a lot of effort for very little gain – and, now that other sweeteners are readily available, most people no longer make watermelon molasses, but I wanted to include a recipe as I felt it was important to document the process.

Where I come from in the south of Ukraine, this is also called watermelon honey, and it was our go-to sweetener back in the day. It would be spread on rye bread, just like honey, or used as a sweetener in desserts and puddings. This is still standard practice in the Caucasus, where the same method has been adapted to make molasses with other locally available fruit, such as plums, mulberries, pomegranates, and sour cherries.

45 lb watermelon
(2-4 watermelons, depending
on size)

Chop the watermelons in half and scoop out the flesh. (The rinds would not have been wasted, either: with the tough outer green layer peeled off, the pale-green pith would be pickled or turned into a sweet preserve. I often donate my watermelon rinds to my mum's chickens!)

Push the watermelon flesh through a large fine-meshed sieve set over a really big stockpot: you should end up with roughly 3½ gallons of juice. Now, if you are making this on your own, put on a really interesting podcast – or, better still, invite friends over to hang out and help you with all the stirring, because you now have to stir the juice continuously with a large wooden spoon for several hours, until it turns into thick, dark molasses. Transfer to a 16-ounce jar with a lid, put on the lid, and store in the fridge for up to 6 months.

Wheat bran and polenta *kvas*

MAKES ENOUGH TO FILL
A 2-QT JAR

This is an ancient way to make a sour fermented liquid for use in broths and soups. *Kvas*, as it is called, is common across Romania and in parts of Ukraine near the border with Romania and Moldova (across the border in Romania, it is known as *borş*). In the Danube Delta, wheat bran and polenta *kvas* is used in a fish soup called *yushka*, and in Besarabia it is added to lamb broths and used as a base for *okroshka*, a chilled summer broth with crunchy vegetables. It also makes a refreshing drink, not unlike kombucha.

Traditionally *kvas* is made in clay pots or wooden barrels, but a jar works well. Fruit-tree leaves and twigs would be used to add wild yeasts and flavor – and if you live in the countryside and have access to unsprayed fruit trees, it's probably fine to use a few of their leaves or twigs here.

2⅓ cups (150g) organic wheat bran

⅔ cup (100g) organic polenta or coarse cornmeal

A few blackcurrant or sour cherry leaves or twigs with leaves – optional

2 sprigs of lovage – optional

In a sterilized 2-quart jar, mix the wheat bran with the polenta or cornmeal and gradually stir in ½ cup of water – you want it to look like porridge. Cover and leave somewhere warm to ferment; in winter, I put it by the radiator. It should start to ferment within 24 hours in the summer, but in winter it may take up to 2 days.

You will know it is ready when the surface starts to look puffy and it is slightly bubbly. Now bring 6 cups of water to a simmer, then take off the heat and let it cool down a little. Pour the still-hot water into the jar – along with the leaves or twigs and the lovage, if using. Cover and leave to ferment somewhere warm.

The fermentation process should restart within 12 hours. Leave it to ferment for 24 hours during the height of summer, or at least 48 hours if the weather is cooler. When you see a white foamy "hat" (called *kushma* in Romanian) on the surface of the *kvas*, it is ready.

Strain the liquid into a sterilized 2-quart jar, but do not throw away the solids – you can add another 1½ cups of wheat bran to them and use it as a starter for your next batch of *kvas*.

The jar of *kvas* will keep in the fridge or a cellar for up to 2 weeks.

Beet *kvas*

MAKES ENOUGH TO FILL
3 X 3-CUP BOTTLES

---

2 tsp sea salt

2 tsp caraway and/or coriander seeds, lightly toasted – optional

1 Tbsp honey

1 oz (2 inches) organic ginger, unpeeled and coarsely grated

1 Tbsp organic whole-grain rye flour or rye starter (page 150)

6 cups lukewarm water

1 lb beets, peeled

Beet *kvas* is an ancient drink, which is also used to add a sour note to borsch and other dishes. My family is totally addicted to its bright, slightly salty, sweet and sour flavor.

Don't be tempted to leave out the flour or starter here. Without it, the *kvas* may become thick and viscous – it's just something that beet does.

Using a mortar and pestle, grind the salt with the seeds, if using, until the salt is finely ground (it's okay if the spices still have a little texture). Transfer to a sterilized 2-quart jar with a lid and add the honey, ginger and flour or rye starter. Now pour in the warm water and whisk until the honey, salt, and flour or starter have dissolved.

Cut your beets either into quarters or ¼-inch dice (it doesn't have to be perfect) and add them to the jar.

Put the lid on the jar and leave at room temperature. Your *kvas* will froth up the next day and should be ready to use in 3 days. When it smells and tastes pleasantly sour and becomes a little fizzy – not unlike kombucha – it is ready.

If you know you will use up the *kvas* within a couple of days, pour it straight from the jar. If you want to keep it for longer, strain the liquid from the jar through a sieve into a jug and pour into three sterilized 3-cup bottles. Store in the fridge or cellar, where it will keep for up to 3 months.

Drink your *kvas* in a similar way to kombucha, or use it in broths and stews to add a sour note.

Once the *kvas* is finished, you can re-use the beet and ginger to make another batch of *kvas*: just add the same amounts of salt, spice, honey, flour or starter, and water as above. Experiment with flavorings, too!

Walnut tincture

MAKES 1 QT

In the village of Vinohradiv, in Transcarpathia, I went to visit a remarkable man called Vasiliy Herbey. He distilled his own spirits and had the most impressive collection of *nastoyanka* or *eaux-de-vie* I have ever seen. He was adamant that they were for medicinal use, but quite apart from any remedial qualities, most of Vasyl's tinctures were incredibly delicious.

The one that really stuck in my mind was made with the hard membranes inside walnut shells. You know when you crack open a walnut, there are those tough partitions that you struggle to separate from the delicious walnut kernels? Do not throw them away; when walnuts are plentiful in winter, collect them, keeping them somewhere dry until you have a serious amount. Then you can steep them in vodka to give you something as delicious as the French *eau-de-vie aux cerneaux*. Alternatively, you could just use hot water to extract the goodness from the walnut membranes: simply pour boiling water over them in a cup or pot and leave to infuse, like tea, before drinking.

Inspired by the hundreds of tinctures we saw in Vasyl's basement, here are some ideas for you to experiment with. All you have to do is take a liter of good-quality vodka and steep a handful (or a jarful in this case) of one the following elements in it for at least a month, after which you can strain it before using:

Walnut partitions

Slices of raw quince

Chestnut flowers

Young garlic scapes

Gentian root

Cornelian cherries

Horseradish

On *fermentatsiya*

Let me tell you about fermentation from the perspective of an Eastern European cook. Come September, especially if you live in the countryside or are an urbanite blessed with a plot or *dacha* (summer house) on the outskirts of the city, there is always a glut of something: a hundred pounds of pink, gnarled tomatoes, or twice the amount of zucchini that threaten to turn into marrows the minute you look away. The same goes for prickly cucumbers, red and green peppers, stout pumpkins, watermelons, and tight heads of young jade-green cabbages. And in southern Ukraine, eggplants multiply and swell until they are picked and packed into huge sacks. All of this might be harvested from just one family's garden, a stone's throw from their summer kitchen.

What you do next is very straightforward. For most vegetables, you stir some salt into a vat of hot water to make a brine, then you let it cool down to room temperature. For the next step – let's take the familiar cucumber as an example – you pop your glut of small cucumbers into a big jar. Then you add a couple of blackcurrant or sour cherry twigs or some horseradish leaves: these provide flavor as well as tannins, which will prevent your crisp veggies from going mushy. For extra flavor, you might add a few frilly umbrellas of dill heads, garlic, peppercorns, allspice berries, mint, celery, or lovage. The brine is then poured over this ikebana-like arrangement, covering it completely. The jar will hang around in a dark corner of the kitchen until the brine grows a playful, frothy hat and becomes opaque.

If not eaten immediately, the jars will be taken down to the cellar. If the pickle will not be used within a few months, the fermentation is stopped completely by draining off the brine and boiling it before pouring it back into the jar – this is then hermetically sealed

>>

with a special lid and boiled. Treated in this way, the pickles will last for a few years.

In order to preserve the abundance of fresh produce, fermenting developed as a matter of necessity in Ukraine, as well as a way of adding flavor. In my family, we were all suckers for the fizz and the pop and the acidic punch on our palate. Anything we could get our hands on would be dropped into a bowl, pot, or barrel of brine. Sometimes the fermenting brine would be regulated with a spritz of vinegar and stabilized with a film of toasted sunflower oil to seal the surface, then away it went into the cellar. Come September or October, there would be hundreds of three-quart jars sitting on the shelves of the summer kitchen, and even more jars in the cellar over the winter months, to tide us over until the first fresh cucumbers were ready to harvest in May.

My looking at these traditional recipes and techniques from the perspective of an outsider (I left Ukraine when I was twelve years old) is something my family finds amusing. I have been bothering them with *fermentatsiya* questions for years now, and every time they just laugh their heads off. It is *kvashennia* in Ukrainian, by the way, from the verb *kvasyty* ("to make sour"); the word "fermentation" sounds quite scientific and alien to them.

Following their time-honored methods, my family in Ukraine never encountered a fermented pickle that went off. Sure, when left for too long, things may have grown a bit sour even for our acid-loving palates, but they never became revolting. This did happen to me, however, when I first tried to pickle in the UK. A few times, I just could not get it right. You see, in the countryside, with its sprawling meadows, vegetable patches, and orchards, the air is full of floating natural yeasts that help things to go sour in a good way, and the fruit and vegetables themselves will often have a fine dusting of favorable yeasts clinging to their skins. What's more, people who do a lot of fermenting develop their own yeast and bacterial "aura" of sorts, called a biome.

So, to help maximize your chances of success, here's what I've found works well in a more urban environment. In Ukraine ferments are generally left open and only covered with cheesecloth for the first few days, but I find it best to immediately seal them with a lid. I normally use jars with lids, or glazed-clay fermentation crocks, but lidded Korean kimchi containers also work a treat. I clean my jars, lids, ladles, and crocks with a mild eco-detergent, then pour boiling water over them in the sink and leave them to drain. That is the extent of the sterilization I do, and it works fine for me. Just be careful not to scald rubber seals with boiling water, and avoid using any aggressively chemical foamy cleaners.

As a rule, non-chlorinated water (either filtered or bottled) works better for the brine, but tap water will generally do. And make sure you use non-iodized salt – I use flaky sea salt, but any sea salt will do just fine.

Adding a little brine from another ferment helps things along (shop-bought sauerkraut brine works well), as does a tablespoon of organic whole-grain rye flour, a little rye starter or some stale rye bread. When fermenting beet or making beet *kvas* without any help from rye bread, starter, or rye flour, your ferment may become thick and viscous. Although it's still safe, this is less than desirable, so do give your beet ferments in particular a helping hand.

For the first few days to a week, leave your ferment somewhere warm. In order to tell how it is doing, look at it closely and give it a sniff. A little bit of what looks like white mold (actually kahm yeast) is nothing to worry about. You can either scoop it off and discard it, or just leave it be – it's harmless.

If the brine looks flat and lifeless, however, or smells repulsive or becomes slimy, or if the ferment develops real white mold, flecked with green or blue, unfortunately this means "game over" and you must throw it away and start again.

When you have a successful ferment, you can then re-use that same jar or crock (without rinsing it) for another batch, as it will already have the good stuff you need to kick-start the process.

>>

In the West today, fermented foods like kimchi and kombucha are hip and have come to be associated with health, well-being, and even affluence. It is not cheap to buy organic produce for preserving – in many cities, unless you are lucky enough to have a vegetable patch or garden, you are unlikely to have access to inexpensive gluts of vegetables and fruit. Of course, nobody ever told my family that fermenting food was good for our health; perhaps we were aware that kombucha (wildly popular and called "Indian fungus" in Eastern Europe) had health benefits, but with the rest of it, we just followed tradition.

Perhaps inevitably, such traditional ways of living are changing, as illustrated by this real-life vignette from last summer. In my aunt's village of Lyubymivka, near Kakhovka, we were having a family lunch in the garden, when I heard my cousin's teenage daughter deliver some news to her mother in a voice full of indignation: "Yes, grandad didn't even call. He showed up with two 20-pound sacks of eggplant, dropped them by the door, and left." My cousin's eyes widened, eyebrows raised, "What the hell am I going to do with them? When do I have the time to preserve 40 pounds of bloody eggplant?" My aunt, frowning, said: "You are ungrateful, and we shall never leave anything more by your front door."

Soon enough, things got jovial again and everyone giggled – but, to me, this encapsulates shifting attitudes and practices. Where my mother's generation saw no problem with preserving large amounts of vegetables and fruit over a weekend, young people are becoming busier and they struggle to find the time. For country-dwelling generations before my mother's, it was normal to cook in vast cauldrons – I mean 3 gallons or more, in massive pots over fire – and no one ever complained about a measly 40-pound eggplant *priezent* in those days.

I find myself torn between the two worlds. I am very keen to preserve traditional knowledge, to encourage people to discover something new and marvel at a different culture, to reap the health benefits and enjoy the incredible flavors of fermented foods. And maybe if someone is reading this in Ukraine, they could find a way to politely return the extra twenty, totally impossible pounds of eggplant, but keep the other twenty and spend a leisurely Sunday with their teenage children preserving them – which is exactly what my cousin did, by the way.

Breakfasts and bites

FROM SUNRISE TO SUNSET

We do not do snacks as such in Ukraine, or at least we didn't use to. You had a substantial breakfast, and the biggest meal of the day was at around one in the afternoon. Supper would be light and early; we rarely ate past 6 p.m. – maybe just a cup of tea and an open sandwich.

In Ukraine, my usual childhood breakfast was simple: a slice of white bread, a slab of cold butter, and a thick piece of Gouda-style cheese, washed down with a sweet black tea with lemon juice. I remember squeezing almost half a lemon into the tea, then stirring in generous spoonfuls of sugar. I'd keep going until I had the perfect balance of sweet and sour, to complement the salty cheese. Another breakfast favorite was dark rye bread and caviar. Not that we were wealthy – nobody was at the time – it was just that my dad knew a guy who managed a fish farm, so a big jar of *malossol* (lightly salted) Oscietra fish eggs was often in our fridge. I loved it spooned on top of so much cold butter that you could mistake it for a slice of cheese. This went particularly well with instant coffee sweetened with condensed milk – somehow we were allowed that as kids!

But there is, of course, much more to Ukrainian breakfasts. A traditional village breakfast might consist of eggs and tomatoes, fried in *salo* (fatty cured pork) until the edges of the pork fat and eggs were equally crispy, and the tomatoes started melting into it all. In Ukrainian Polisia, a marshy region stretching along Ukraine's northern border, people often have mushroom broth for breakfast. And I am with them, being a proponent of eating the previous night's leftovers – borsch or chicken soup are among my favorite breakfasts.

Mum often made buckwheat porridge, cooking the toasted grains in sweetened milk. In many parts of the country, pumpkin rice porridge is served with melted butter – or, in Poltava, in central Ukraine, with homemade evaporated milk.

There is also a lot of crossover between meal genres, so to speak. Some of the recipes in this chapter can also be served as *zakusky*, pre-dinner snacks. And some of the savory dishes would not feel out of place as part of a bigger feast. Sweet pancakes can be eaten as a dessert, and the savory ones stuffed with chicken are perfect for picnics or school lunches. I often make the puffed omelette for dinner when I want something light, and burnt eggplant butter slathered on a piece of bread is good even at midnight.

"Rock and roll" pancakes

SERVES 7-8
(MAKES 14-16 PANCAKES)

2 eggs

2 cups whole milk

½ tsp sea salt

1 Tbsp superfine sugar

1-2 Tbsp vegetable oil

2 cups (250g) all-purpose flour

⅓ cup boiling water

1 stick of unsalted butter and maple syrup, honey, or jam, to serve

I grew up eating these pancakes: either sweet ones, pretty much drowned in butter and sugar or filled with vanilla-scented curd cheese and raisins; or a savory version, stuffed with some leftover chicken and mushrooms (page 88). They are thin, but soft and almost spongy, and very "moreish." Adding a splash of hot water to the batter is a trick I learned from my mum – this precooks the flour slightly, resulting in a lacy, melt-in-the-mouth pancake. Another of her tricks is to sit a whole stick of butter on top of each one when it comes out of the pan, leaving it to melt into the hot pancake while you make the next one.

My son Sasha has christened these "rock and roll" pancakes, because of the way my mum rolls them up to make them easier to eat and to stop any of the precious butter and syrup from escaping. And the rock bit has to do with the fact that...they rock!

Sasha is these pancakes' biggest fan, to the point of obsession – something he might just have inherited from me. One harsh, rainy April morning in 2012, close to my due date, I woke up at 9 a.m. (late-pregnancy lie in!) with an overwhelming desire for these very pancakes. Alone in the house, I got up to make them and hobbled to the kitchen. Well, I must have produced so much oxytocin thinking about my imminent pancake breakfast that my labor started, and Sash was born five hours later.

In a bowl, whisk together the eggs, milk, salt, sugar, and 1 tablespoon of the oil. Gradually add the flour, whisking constantly, until you have a smooth batter – the consistency should be a tad thicker than heavy cream. Now add the hot water in one shot, whisking it in briskly.

Have two large plates ready: one for buttering, and another for rolling up the cooked pancakes for small (or big) hands to come and collect. Have that unwrapped stick of butter handy too!

Now heat a 7-inch nonstick frying pan over medium heat. wBecause you have added some oil to the batter, you shouldn't need to grease it, but if your pan is a bit temperamental, add a little oil and use some paper towels to wipe it around the pan.

Pour a ladleful (roughly ¼ cup) of the batter into the center of the hot pan, swirling it around so the batter covers the base in a thin layer. Let the pancake cook for about a minute, until you see tiny bubbles appearing on the surface and the edges are going brown.

Gently lift the sides with a spatula and your fingertips and carefully flip it over. The pancakes will be delicate and thin, so this may take a little practice! Cook for another 10–15 seconds, no more – if they're overcooked, they'll lose that luscious texture.

Lift the cooked pancake onto one of the plates, plonk the stick of butter on top of it, and leave it there while you cook the next pancake. When that one is ready, slide it out of the pan onto the other plate, then transfer the butter onto it. Drizzle some maple syrup, honey, or jam over the first pancake, then fold in the sides and bottom and roll it up just like you would a burrito.

Now repeat the process with the rest of the pancakes. If you like, you can cook half of the batter and keep the rest in the fridge for the next day. Or stop the extravagant buttering of the pancakes after the first one or two and leave the rest naked to make the recipe on the next page...

Pancakes with mushrooms and chicken

SERVES 4-6
(MAKES 56 TINY PANCAKES
OR 14 BIGGER ONES)

This recipe is a tribute to my late grandmother, Vera, who passed away while I was writing this book. Originally from Siberia, she lived in Ukraine for sixty years, two-thirds of her remarkable life – and, despite the harsh conditions she was forced to endure at various stages in her life, she remained kind and strong. She always insisted that these stuffed *blinchiki* (little blinis) should be bite-sized – I think she enjoyed devoting her time and concentration to making them for us. When she stayed at our house during the summer, at the end of each day she would ceremoniously close the kitchen door and declare: "The buffet is shut!" It was her way of saying that we were not to ask for any more food…but we knew that if we did ask, she would still give us something.

These pancakes are perfect for picnics or lunchboxes – make in advance and keep in the fridge for up to 3 days. But I think they are best gently refried in a little butter and served with yogurt. To make them vegetarian, leave out the chicken and double the amount of mushrooms. For extra flavor, you could also cook some coarsely grated carrot, shredded kale, or thinly sliced leeks with the onions (you will need about 1½ pounds of filling for 14 pancakes).

---

14 x 7-inch-wide pancakes
(page 86)

2 Tbsp vegetable oil, plus a
little more if needed

4 small onions, finely chopped

8 oz mushrooms, roughly
chopped

8 oz leftover poached or
roast chicken (about 1⅓ cups)

Sea salt and black pepper

Put the pancakes into a neat pile – and, if you don't mind the fiddly process ahead, cut them into quarters, to give you 56 small, triangular pancakes. Otherwise just leave them whole.

Heat the oil in a frying pan over medium-low heat and add the onions with a pinch of salt – this will draw out the moisture and help to stop them from burning. Cook them for about 10 minutes, until golden, stirring from time to time. Sometimes I use a cartouche to help speed up the process: cut out a circle of baking parchment about the same size as the pan, wet it, and place it on top of the onions, so they steam-fry. When the onions are ready, transfer them to a food processor.

Add a bit more oil to the pan if it seems dry and turn up the heat to medium-high. Throw in the mushrooms and cook (in batches if your pan is not huge), stirring occasionally, for about 5–7 minutes, until brown, then transfer to the food processor. Add the chicken to the food processor as well, then blitz everything to a paste. Season to taste with salt and pepper.

If you're making 56 small pancakes, place 1 teaspoon of the filling at the wider end of each triangular pancake, fold in the sides and roll it up. Place it, seam side down, on a plate or into a container. If you're making 14 bigger pancakes, use 1½ tablespoons of filling for each one, then fold in the sides and roll up like a burrito. Repeat with the rest of the pancakes and filling.

Buckwheat drop scones

SERVES 4-5
(MAKES 8-10 DROP SCONES)

I have come across a myriad of old Ukrainian recipes that use a natural sourdough leaven called *opara* to make pancakes, and buckwheat flour also features in many of them. Zinoviya Klynovetska, one of Ukraine's pioneering food writers, has a recipe for what she calls *lyapuny*, or buckwheat flour pancakes, in her seminal 1913 *Dishes and Drinks of Ukraine*. These drop scones were partly inspired by that recipe and partly by British pikelets, cousins of the crumpet. If you want to make them the traditional way, you'll have to mix the batter the day before, as the sourdough needs to ferment overnight.

6 Tbsp (100g) rye starter (page 150)
or
Half a ¼-oz packet fast-action dried yeast

¾ cup (100g) buckwheat flour

¾ cup (100g) bread flour

½ cup + 2 Tbsp whole milk

½ cup + 2 Tbsp lukewarm water

½ tsp baking soda

1 Tbsp honey

½ tsp sea salt

2-3 Tbsp vegetable oil

Butter and maple syrup or honey, to serve

If you're using rye starter, put it in a bowl and stir in the buckwheat and bread flours, milk, and water to make a thick batter – it should fall off the spoon freely. Cover with plastic wrap and leave at room temperature overnight.

If you're using dried yeast, make the batter an hour or so before you need it. In a bowl, mix the yeast with the buckwheat and bread flours, then gradually add the milk and water, stirring to make a thick batter – it should fall off the spoon freely. Cover with plastic wrap and leave to stand for 15 minutes–1 hour.

When it's ready, the batter should look lively and bubbly. Stir in the baking soda, honey, and salt and mix well.

Heat 1–2 tablespoons of the oil in a nonstick frying pan over medium-low heat. When the oil is hot, add 2 tablespoonfuls of the batter to make a drop scone. Depending on the size of your pan, you might be able to cook a couple at a time, but if you've used rye starter, cook a tester one first – if it is too fluid and difficult to flip, stir in a touch more flour before cooking the rest.

Fry on the first side until the top looks set and has holes forming, like a crumpet, and the underside is golden and crispy. Use a spatula to flip it, then cook for another 15–20 seconds. Remove from the pan and keep warm while you cook the rest, adding a little more oil to the pan as needed.

To serve, slather the side with the holes with butter and maple syrup or honey.

Puffed omelette with broccoli

SERVES 2 FOR BREAKFAST,
OR 1 FOR A LIGHT LUNCH
OR DINNER

4 oz broccoli

1 Tbsp canola or vegetable oil

1 Tbsp butter

3 eggs

½ cup yogurt or whole milk

Sea salt and black pepper

Ukrainians have a special love for sour milk products, eulogizing *smetana*, a type of sour cream that is made all over Central and Eastern Europe. A really good-quality cultured cream or crème fraîche can do wonders for a dish, enriching it at the same time as providing tart freshness.

My mum makes what I call a puffed omelette using *smetana*, and there is something almost Japanese about its delicate, custardy texture. To achieve this, use good-quality sour cream, crème fraîche, or whole milk; I more often go for thick, full-fat yogurt. This omelette is extremely light and really satisfying to make, and you can substitute almost any other vegetable for the broccoli: thickly sliced tomatoes or cauliflower, spinach, chopped spring greens, green beans, or green onions. Eat it with bread or toast for a hearty breakfast or brunch, or with a side salad if you want a light lunch or dinner.

Cut the florets off the broccoli, then trim off the tougher outer layer of the stalk. Cut the sweet inner core of the stalk into slices about the same size as the florets. (I often give these to my son to eat raw while he's waiting for his breakfast, but you can also use them in the omelette.)

Heat the oil and butter in a 7-inch nonstick frying pan, ideally one with a lid; otherwise a makeshift lid, such as a plate, will do. Add the broccoli – including the stalks, if using – and start browning it over medium heat.

Meanwhile, whisk the eggs with the yogurt or milk and season quite generously with salt and pepper. If you have time, use a handheld mixer – you want the egg mixture to become really voluminous.

When your broccoli is nice and browned – "rosy-cheeked," as Ukrainians would say – turn up the heat to high and gently pour in the egg mixture. Immediately cover the pan and cook for 1–2 minutes, then lower the heat to the minimum possible and cook for another minute or two. When you lift the lid you will be met by the flamboyant creature that is our puffed omelette: it should have a light, fluffy texture – and if you used yogurt, a pleasantly sour note.

Pumpkin rice porridge

SERVES 4-6

1½-lb baking pumpkin (1 lb peeled weight), cut into ¾-inch chunks

¾ cup short-grain rice, washed

1 heaping tsp sea salt

½ cup whole milk

1 tsp vanilla extract

1½ Tbsp unsalted butter

¼ cup honey or maple syrup, plus extra to serve

Evaporated milk, to serve – optional

Pumpkins are very rarely used in Ukrainian savory dishes – in fact, in the countryside they are often fed to farm animals, but this sweet pumpkin rice porridge is something I grew up with, and it's a real favorite in many regions. My grandmother used to boil the pumpkin in milk, but I find that it's all too easy for the milk to catch and burn, so I prefer to use water. My parents' generation usually sweetened their rice porridge with sugar (not necessarily traditional, as sugar was a luxury for my grandparents' generation and the ones before them), but I tend to go for honey or maple syrup instead.

Put the cut-up pumpkin into a saucepan and cover with 3 cups of water. Bring to a boil, then simmer for about 20 minutes, or until the pumpkin is very soft. Add the rice and salt to the pan and cook over low heat for about 10 minutes, until the rice is just cooked.

Add the milk and vanilla extract, then mash the pumpkin into the liquid with a potato masher. Cook the porridge for another 10 minutes, stirring so it doesn't catch and burn on the bottom of the pan – add a splash more water or milk if it starts looking dry.

When the rice is soft and the porridge is thick and creamy, stir through the butter and honey or maple syrup.

If you feel like the porridge could be sweeter, drizzle over some extra honey or syrup once it is in your bowl. Serve with evaporated milk, if desired.

Curd cheese with green onions, herbs, and radishes

SERVES 4

12 radishes and/or other crunchy vegetables (carrots, cucumbers, Belgian endive, etc.)

7 oz curd cheese, cottage cheese, or similar

2 green onions, thinly sliced

Handful of soft herbs (I like to use dill, cilantro, purple basil, and tarragon), finely chopped

Sea salt and black pepper

Bread, to serve

This is a bit of a non-recipe, unless you fancy making your own *syr* curd cheese (page 338). But, just as the French love spreading butter on their radishes and Italians enjoy dipping radishes and other raw vegetables into *bagna cauda*, Ukrainians and Poles love radishes with a flavored curd cheese. Homemade *syr* is the most popular, but you could use cottage cheese, a mixture of feta and ricotta, or feta whipped with a little crème fraîche. Or simply buy some freshly made ricotta or goat's curd and you will come very close to the real thing: a crunchy seasonal vegetable, plus some sweet-tasting cheese flavored with punchy green onions and whatever herbs you have around – use any or all of chives, dill, basil, tarragon, cilantro, chervil, and wild garlic.

I have fond memories of snacking on this in a summer kitchen in Lviv, listening to 1920s Polish music on an ancient gramophone. My dapper new friend Kostyantyn Kovalyshyn, wearing a colorful shirt and a smoking cap, explained that it is called *avanturka* ("hustler's snack") because you can prepare it stealthily and quickly when unexpected guests arrive.

Trim and clean the vegetables. If using any larger vegetables, cut them into bite-sized pieces.

Now simply mix your curd cheese with the green onions, herbs, and salt and pepper to taste.

Serve with bread as part of a breakfast, or instead of crudités before a meal.

Whipped garlic *salo* on rye

SERVES 10

A bite of dark rye bread with melting garlicky fat, followed by the smooth heat of chilled vodka and a pickle chaser works a treat to get the conversation flowing before dinner. You can also just serve the garlic-spiked *salo* (cured pork fat) with your bread basket instead of butter – it is that delicious. And a tablespoonful of it is great whisked through a winter borsch (page 136) at the very end of cooking.

If you're short of time but still want to serve some *salo* as a premeal snack, you don't have to do the whipping bit – simply freeze the *salo* or *lardo* until solid, then slice it very thinly and pop it on top of thinly sliced toasted rye bread.

7-oz slab of *salo* (page 338) or *lardo*

2 large garlic cloves, peeled *or*
2 whole bulbs and stems of wild garlic (flowers kept for garnish), chopped

Handful of chopped fresh herbs, such as dill, cilantro, and parsley

Sea salt – optional

Rye bread, thinly sliced

Slice the hard skin off the *salo* or *lardo* and discard it. Cut the fat into chunks, then blitz in a food processor until smooth. Add the garlic cloves or wild garlic and the herbs and pulse until incorporated. Taste and add a touch of salt if you think it needs it.

Serve on thin slices of fresh or toasted rye bread.

Any leftover whipped *salo* will keep in a jar in the fridge for months, and it can also be frozen for up to 4 months.

Odesan *zakuska*

SERVES 10

This is a retro Jewish classic from Odesa – some call it Jewish *zakuska* (a kind of hors d'oeuvre). I love it, and often serve it as a vegetarian canapé instead of whipped garlic *salo* (page 102). What's not to like about garlicky cheese, mayo, and egg on a bit of rye bread? You could also serve this on tomato slices in summer or thinly sliced raw beets in winter – add a bit of finely grated horseradish to the cheesy mixture for the latter.

I often use Gruyère or Cheddar to make my *zakuska*, but any tasty hard cheese will work. One time when I was cooking near the Welsh border, for a Ukrainian charity dinner, I had surprise vegetarian guests, and some local Hereford Hop worked a treat!

4 oz Gruyère or similar cheese

2 hard-boiled eggs, shelled

2 garlic cloves, peeled

¼ cup mayonnaise

Rye bread, thinly sliced

Black pepper

Grate the cheese on the coarse side of a box grater into a bowl. Do the same with the eggs. Finely grate the garlic into the mayonnaise and mix, then gently fold the mayo through the cheese and the eggs.

Cut the slices of bread into triangles and top with the cheesy mixture. Grind some pepper over and serve.

Burnt eggplant butter on tomato toasts

SERVES 6

---

1 large eggplant

1½ Tbsp best-quality butter, softened

6 slices sourdough bread

1 large garlic clove, peeled and cut in half

2 ripe tomatoes, cut in half

Finely chopped fresh herbs, such as dill, basil, cilantro – optional

Sea salt and black pepper

Don't be fooled by the modern-sounding title – I first found a delightfully simple version of this recipe in Olga Franko's brilliant 1929 book called *Practical Cooking*. I was intrigued by the way that, throughout the book, the Ukrainian terms for eggplant and tomatoes seemed very confused: the word for eggplant is "purple tomato" and for tomato "red eggplant"!

If you haven't tried eggplant with butter before, this will be a revelation. It is delicious and silky and makes for the best starter or sharing dish. Add some fresh herbs too, if you have them.

You need to blacken and cook the eggplant until it collapses, as you would for baba ganoush. The best result comes from doing this over the smoldering coals of a barbecue, but you can also do it over an open flame if you have a gas stove: set the eggplant directly over a medium flame and keep turning it with your tongs every 5 minutes – it should take about 10–15 minutes. Alternatively, you can roast it in a 425°F oven or under a hot broiler for about 20 minutes, turning occasionally.

When the eggplant is charred on the outside and really soft inside, set it aside on a plate until it is just cool enough to handle. Pour off the liquid that will have come out of the eggplant into a bowl, then use your fingers to peel off the skin – don't worry if some of it doesn't come off, it will only add to the flavor. Add the eggplant flesh to the bowl containing the liquid and mash with a fork. While it is still warm, whisk in the butter with the fork and add some salt and pepper, then taste – it should be well seasoned and taste of comfort, like baba ganoush's Ukrainian third cousin.

Grill your slices of bread on a griddle pan (or toast them), then rub first with the garlic, followed by the tomatoes - as you would for Spanish *pan con tomate*. Now spoon some of the eggplant butter on top. Garnish with some finely chopped soft herbs, if you like, and serve.

If there is any eggplant butter leftover, it will keep for up to a week in the fridge.

Eggs with horseradish mayonnaise and wild garlic

SERVES 4-6

---

6 eggs

Handful of wild garlic flowers or dill, to garnish

HORSERADISH MAYONNAISE

2 egg yolks (freeze the leftover whites to make meringues)

1 Tbsp Dijon or other smooth mustard

¾ oz horseradish root, peeled and finely grated
or
1 Tbsp jarred horseradish sauce

Juice of 1 lemon

½ cup canola or any mild-flavored vegetable oil

Sea salt and black pepper

For years I felt a little embarrassed about enjoying wonderfully old-school dishes like this one, but now I am a little older, I see no shame in any of them. There is something so delicious about egg mayonnaise, I implore you to bring it back. If you don't want to make your own mayonnaise, you can always use store-bought – you will need about ½ cup – and then just stir through the horseradish and lemon juice.

These eggs are traditionally served during Easter as part of a bigger feast. If you want to make them when wild garlic is not in season, simply use another soft herb – you can never go wrong with dill when you make Ukrainian dishes.

The following instructions are for those (including myself, admittedly!) who always have to check how to boil a bloody egg. I can make intricate dumplings, but the prospect of boiling eggs always makes me anxious. So, for hard-boiled eggs with a soft yolk center, put the eggs into a pan of cold water. Watch them, for as soon as the water comes to a rolling boil, you must turn the heat down to low and set a timer for 4 minutes. When the time is up, drain the eggs and submerge them in cold water. (For perfect soft-boiled eggs, set your timer for 3 minutes.)

For the mayonnaise, put the egg yolks into a medium bowl. Add the mustard, horseradish, lemon juice, and a generous pinch of salt, then whisk well. Now pour your oil into a jug and slowly start trickling it into the bowl, whisking all the time. When all the oil has been incorporated, you should end up with a delightful pillowy horseradish mayo. Taste it again, adding more salt and some pepper if the flavor seems underwhelming.

Shell the eggs and cut them in half, then spoon a little horseradish mayo on top and sprinkle with wild garlic flowers or dill.

Broths and soups

A NOURISHING BOWL

There is nothing Ukrainians love more than broths. When I say broth, I mean a clear soup with bits in it, rather than a creamed soup. When my mum visits me in London, she must have either broth or soup every single day. I imagine she is not the only Ukrainian mum with such specific demands, and I wonder if it all comes down to borsch.

Borsch is both a national treasure and a source of acute pride. It is not just considered to be a starter, but a meal in itself.

The youngest of six children, my mum learned how to make borsch when she was seven years old. One particularly vicious winter, my grandmother Lyusia succumbed to angina and, as her older children were already at university or working, it was left to my mother to make dinner. Running between Grandmother's bedside and the kitchen, she put coal into the *pich* oven, stood on a stool to slice all the vegetables (most likely with a maddeningly blunt knife!), filled the big stockpot with water, seasoned the broth, and managed to make a very passable borsch.

As for me, I was not the most robust child, and I was also a very peculiar eater. I ate things like chicken gizzards with no problem, but would often get fixated on one dish, and persuade my mum to make it for as many as seven days in a row. It could be, say, buckwheat, chicken liver, and onions... for seven days. Then it might be chicken soup for five days, and so on. One time I got a really nasty cold, and I'll never forget the dreadful day when my mum tried to make this and that for me, and I just kept refusing all of it, while crying desperate, frustrated tears. Mum must have looked so upset herself that Dad flew to our rescue. He threw a whole, peeled onion, a bay leaf, and salt into a saucepan of water, followed by some diced potato. Finally, in went some chopped hard-boiled eggs, a little butter, and dill. Well, I promptly ate two whole bowls of this "soup." We called it *papskiy supchyk* ("dad's little soup") and after that fateful day my dad often made it for me, even when I wasn't ill.

Many years later, when I was reading about the Jewish food of Besarabia, I came across a description of exactly this soup – our *papskiy supchyk* – in the context of a meal eaten during *Pesakh* (Passover). It made me smile that my dad had somehow come up with a version of this comforting soup by complete accident. But perhaps it wasn't entirely by accident, for this is what Ukrainians and other Eastern Europeans excel at: creating a nourishing meal, full of flavor, out of nothing more than a few ingredients and water. Try some of the exquisite soups in this chapter and you'll see what I mean.

On borsch

A whole book could be written on borsch. It is eaten from the formerly Prussian Kaliningrad all the way through the Caucasus and into Iran to the west, south into Central Asia, and right across to Sakhalin and Kamchatka to the east. However, I am not afraid to claim borsch here as Ukrainian. It is *the* Ukrainian traditional dish – an unblended soup that involves beet and as many as seventy other ingredients, depending on region, season, occasion, and taste. Apart from its staggering international range and diversity, borsch is also a constantly evolving dish, one that invites curious and creative cooks to experiment, adapt, and adjust their recipe. I have heard stories that begin with "I'm Czech, but my Crimean Jewish grandmother…"; "Our borsch, made in the Manitoba Mennonite tradition, by way of western Ukraine, is…"; "My Iranian dad loved this version of my Russian mother's borsch…" The variations are endless.

Borsch wasn't only cooked at home, either. Come the revolution, it was commonly served in Soviet canteens. I love this description from Teffi, a hugely underrated Russian writer who, along with other intellectuals, was forced to flee St. Petersburg, via Kyiv and Odesa, for Paris. In *Memories*, written in 1926, she recalls her first impressions of Kyiv: "Kiev! The station is crammed with people and the whole place smells of borsch. The new arrivals are in the buffet, partaking of the culture of a free country. They slurp away with deep concentration. With their elbows jutting out to either side as if to ward off any encroachment, they seem like eagles hovering over their prey. But how can anyone behave otherwise? …Your subconscious sticks out your elbows and sends your eyes on stalks. 'What if an unfamiliar, vile spoon reaches over my shoulder,' it says to itself, 'and takes a scoop for the needs of the proletariat?'"

>>

But the ancient precursor of borsch had very little to do with the soup we know today. As far back as AD 900, at the dawn of Kyivan Rus, early Slavonic people reportedly made it with sour-tasting hogweed. Later on, goosefoot (from the amaranth family), then beet leaves, and eventually the root itself began to take center stage. The origins of the name can be traced back to *buriak*, meaning "beet" in Ukrainian, and etymologically linked to the ancient Slavic *bor* for "red." However, there are questions surrounding the issue of color. In the past, on the territory of present-day Ukraine, borsch would not actually have been red until tomatoes came into play in the mid-1850s. Before that, beet borsch would have been seen as "black," and spring versions that made use of young nettles, sorrel, and beet leaves were named "white," "yellow," or "green," depending on the region.

The color conundrum goes beyond these historical discrepancies. My maternal grandmother, Lyusia, originally from Besarabia, was resolute about the "correct" color of borsch. It had to be a deep and dusty rose color, imparted by the pink flesh of the giant local tomatoes. The beet also had to be of a specific variety, something labeled as *borschoviy buriak* at the bazaar. These "borsch beets" were candy pink and white, similar to the Chioggia varieties we sometimes see in shops and markets nowadays. For Lyusia, it came down to aesthetics: she could not stand the thought of potatoes and other vegetables being stained the same red or, even worse, a purple color – there had to be a varied color palette. Of course there was a reason beyond "eating the rainbow" for her unswerving opinions on borsch. Borsch was best *her way* because it was intrinsic to the environment she lived in: the sandy soil produced paler beets and the local tomatoes grew into juicy, deep pink, gnarled monsters.

Lyusia wouldn't have liked to hear it, but the earliest versions of borsch would have been deep purple, as fermented beet *kvas* was – and still is in some places – used to add color. More importantly, *kvas* serves as a souring

agent, and this brings us from color to flavor. Borsch has developed into a dish with multi-layered, complex flavors: sweet and deeply savory, often a little hot – but sourness is what defines an excellent borsch today. In the south of Ukraine, this would usually be derived from fresh tomatoes in summer, and in winter from a fermented tomato pulp called *mors*. Closer to the Polish border, fresh or fermented apples would be used to lend acidity, and in central Ukraine, raw sour cherries, unripe apricots, mirabelle plums, and green strawberries might have been added in the past. In Romania, Moldova, and the neighboring areas of southwest Ukraine, cornmeal and wheat bran would be mixed with water and sour cherry branches and left to go fizzy, earthy, and intensely sour. Of course, borsch-making is not always steeped in tradition, and vinegar and lemon juice as souring agents also figure in modern recipes – even ketchup, a new discovery for those who migrated to the USA, has been adapted with glee.

The stock, more often than not, would once have been vegetarian in farming households, with most of the savory, "umami" flavor coming from dried mushrooms, especially in the north and northwest of the country.

When meat was used, pork, beef, rooster, and duck were popular choices. Lyusia favored pork ribs, but my mother liked beef brisket or oxtail – the latter came disconcertingly long, thin and whole, and would fall apart in the tall stockpot after hours of cooking. In the city of Dnipro, I also tried a borsch made using slow-cooked pork preserved for winter (*tushonka*). Using preserved meat in this way made hasty preparation possible when unexpected guests arrived. My mother sometimes used offal, usually chicken hearts and gizzards, to make a quick stock for borsch. In Sumy, north of Poltava, liver is added to the soup.

And, of course, there might be bones – if you are lucky, marrow bones, as in this description from Mikhail Bulgakov's *The Master and Margarita*: "Nikanor Ivanovich poured himself a tumbler of vodka, drank it, poured another, drank that, scooped three pieces of

>>

pickled herring with his fork...and then the doorbell rang. Pelagea Antonovna was just bringing in a steaming soup tureen, one glance at which was enough to reveal that inside the thick, volcanic borsch was hidden the most delicious thing in the world – a marrow bone... His wife ran into the hallway, and Nikanor Ivanovich dragged the bone out of its fiery lake towards him with a ladle. It was quivering and split down the middle."

By way of contrast, the Russian royal courts of the early nineteenth century served a heightened version: "Tsar's borsch" might be made from three stocks – veal, morel, goose and prune – with sour cherries used for acidity before tomatoes became de rigueur.

If no other meat was available, there would always be a bit of "old" salted pork fat in the cellar. Too pungent to be eaten on dark rye bread with shots of vodka, it would be pounded with raw garlic and stirred through the borsch at the very end of cooking. I like to think of it as a Ukrainian fish sauce of sorts. Saying that, in the Kherson region, where I come from, little goby fish used to be butterflied, salted, and dried in the sun, then pounded into a rough paste and used in winter to add depth of flavor and extra nutrition to borsch. My grandmother Lyusia would also fry these same fish, which tasted like crayfish, and add them to bowls of borsch just before serving.

Along the Danube River, in Vylkove, Russian Old Believers (who moved there in the early eighteenth century to escape persecution) still cook borsch in the church for the whole of the community. In the past, sturgeon heads and cartilage were included, but today carp more often takes its place. Such borsch is called *nastorchak* – "the one that sticks out" – presumably referring to the fish heads! And elvers (young eels) once found their way into borsch in Ukrainian Polisia, a long stretch of woods and marshes in the north of the country, before the eel population became severely depleted.

As for vegetables, *zasmazhka*, a base of slowly fried onion and carrot similar to Italian *soffritto*, is responsible for bringing sweetness to Ukrainian-style borsch in most regions. Some may also add a little sugar, but my purist family have always relied on gentle frying to coax the natural sugars out of finely diced onion and thinly sliced carrot. Mum never used any extra oil, she would just skim some fat from the surface of whatever meat stock was on the go and

>>

slick it into a frying pan. Parsnips would be used in the Vinnytsia region, and earthy celery root and turnips might make an appearance in the north. In summer, red bell peppers are very popular all over Ukraine – in fact, to me, a summer borsch is incomplete without them.

Traditionally, in my hometown, smaller varieties of tomatoes would be cut in half, covered with cheesecloth, and left to dry, alongside the goby fish, in the blistering sun. These sun-dried tomatoes would then be pounded and added to borsch when fresh ones were out of season. In the Dnipro area, on the border with eastern Ukraine, they traditionally added eggplant to their borsch, which both thickened it and added an extra umami note.

Or the sweetness can come from fruit. In the region of Poltava, prunes and whole pears, slow-dried in wood-fired ovens, are used in poultry and pork borsches. Dried fruit would have originally been added to provide extra nutrients in winter, and this also lent a unique smoky-sweet flavor and a deep "black" color to local borsches.

Next let us consider the consistency of borsch. My grandmother Lyusia was a staunch proponent of an intensely thick borsch. She firmly believed that you should be able to stand a spoon upright in the pan, wedged among all the vegetables and red kidney beans. For years I followed her dogma and childishly turned up my nose at borsches that were anything but a semi-stew. Until, that is, a few years ago, when I tried and fell in love with a Christmas borsch influenced by neighboring Poland – a clear, delicate, crimson consommé with small dumplings called *vushka* ("little ears"), stuffed with wild mushrooms and sauerkraut.

The seasons are responsible for a lot of borsch variations. In spring, heavy tubers might be swapped for young beet tops, sorrel, wild garlic, nettles, soft herbs, green onions, and, more rarely, garden peas, resulting in a much gentler and thinner beast called green borsch, often enriched with a garnish of chopped hard-boiled eggs. Ice-cold, bright-red beet broth emerges in the warmer months, perhaps with chopped radishes and cucumbers for crunch, and kefir or buttermilk to add the desired sour note.

Which brings me to the final touches, for a dash of aromatic freshness and even a little heat. Dill and parsley are the most ubiquitous finishing herbs – either fresh or packed with salt into jars to be kept for winter – but in parts of western Ukraine, near the Polish border, there may be speckles of wild thyme and marjoram. A lot of Ukrainians claim not to enjoy spicy food, but chiles will often be added to the stockpot. And in the summer, whole green onions and raw garlic might be served alongside a bowl of borsch, to be bitten into between spoonfuls.

Sour cream is generally added, either whisked into the whole pot or served on the table, but I tend to leave it out – the creamy sourness is lovely, but I feel it dilutes the flavor. A traditional borsch accompaniment all over Ukraine is *pampushky*: these sweet and savory fluffy buns, baked side by side or steamed, are covered with an herb and garlic oil called *salamakha* while still hot. But I can never resist a slice or two of traditional crusty, flat, dark rye bread covered in coriander and caraway seeds.

Perhaps the reason borsch has cemented itself as a national treasure in Ukraine is precisely because it is so multifaceted and readily adaptable. This has enabled it to evolve over the centuries and find avid proponents in every corner of the country and across the globe without losing its essence and its roots. For every Ukrainian, borsch triggers deep memories and feelings of kinship. A delectable meal in itself, a bowl of borsch represents family and sustenance, and connects us to home, wherever we find ourselves.

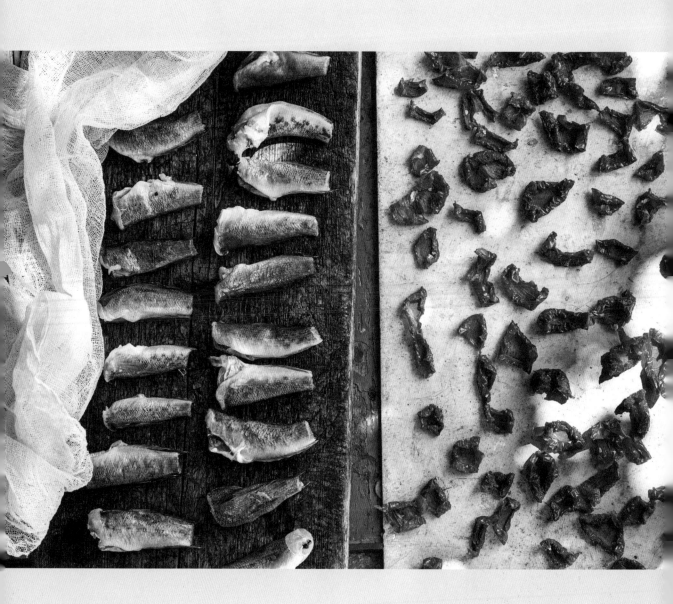

Christmas borsch with mushroom dumplings

SERVES 2-4

1¾ oz dried porcini mushrooms

1 cup hot water

1 onion, skin on, halved

2 celery ribs, roughly chopped

2 carrots, scrubbed and roughly chopped

¼ celery root, peeled and chopped

1 beet, peeled and grated

¼–½ cup beet *kvas* (page 68), to taste – optional

1 Tbsp honey – optional

Sea salt and black pepper

DUMPLINGS

2⅓ cups (300g) '00' pasta flour or 2½ cups (300g) all-purpose flour

1 egg

3 Tbsp butter

1 Tbsp olive or vegetable oil

3 shallots, finely diced

5 oz portobello or cremini mushrooms, finely diced

3 oz sauerkraut

Unlike the thick, almost stew-like borsches I grew up with, this is a rather elegant affair, a beet and mushroom consommé of sorts, and it comes from western Ukraine, near the Polish border. I love adding a splash of beet *kvas* to intensify the color even more. The delicate dumplings, which are often filled with sauerkraut and mushrooms, resemble ears, hence the name, *borsch z vushkamy* ("borsch with little ears"). This festive-looking soup makes a perfect starter for Christmas or a dinner party – or, with a few more dumplings, a meal for two.

Soak the dried porcini in the hot water for about 30 minutes.

Meanwhile, put the onion, celery, carrots and celery root into a large stockpot and add 2 quarts of cold water. Bring to a boil, then lower the heat and simmer for about 50 minutes. Add the grated beet and season the stock really well with salt, then take it off the heat.

Strain the dried mushrooms, reserving the soaking liquid (leaving behind any sandy residue) and add it to the stock. Finely chop the reconstituted mushrooms and set aside to use in the dumpling filling later.

Let the stock stand, so the flavors marry, while you make the dumplings.

To make the dumpling dough, put the flour in a mixing bowl. Beat the egg with ½ cup of water, then gradually add this to the flour, mixing with a spoon and then with your hands to bring together into a dough. Knead on a well-floured surface until you have a firm, elastic dough. Cover with a clean kitchen towel or wrap in plastic wrap and let it rest for about 20 minutes.

For the filling, heat the butter and oil in a medium frying pan over medium-low heat. Add the shallots and a pinch of salt. When you hear them starting to sizzle, cover with a wet cartouche (circle of baking parchment) and keep cooking gently over lowish heat, stirring from time to time, until the shallots soften and deepen in color. Add the portobello or cremini mushrooms, turn up the heat to medium, and cook until they also soften and reduce in volume. Add the reconstituted porcini mushrooms and cook for another few minutes. Finally, add the sauerkraut and cook for another 5 minutes. Check the filling for seasoning – it should be very well seasoned, so add more salt and some pepper if you think it needs it. Transfer to a bowl and leave to cool completely.

To make the dumplings, roll out the dough into a thin sheet, as you would for ravioli. I do this with a rolling pin on a well-floured surface, but you could use a pasta machine if you want.

Cut the sheet of dough into 3¼-inch squares: you should end up with about 14 squares. Place a teaspoon of the filling in the middle of each square. Now fold in half to make a triangle, pressing the edges together firmly and making sure no air is trapped inside. Join the two pointy ends together, again pressing firmly, so the dumplings look like little sailor hats or ears. Place the dumplings on a flour-dusted tray or plate.

Strain the vegetables out of the stock and then either purée them for another use or compost them. If using *kvas*, add it gradually, to taste: I sometimes balance the flavor with a spoonful of honey if it seems too sharp. What you're after is a flavorsome, sweet and sour, deep crimson, clear consommé.

So as not to make the consommé starchy, cook the dumplings in a separate saucepan of boiling, salted water for about 2 minutes – they are ready when they float to the top. Place a few dumplings in each soup bowl and pour the gorgeous red beet broth over.

Nettle, sorrel, and wild garlic soup

SERVES 6

---

2 Tbsp canola or olive oil

1 onion, cut into ½-inch dice

2 carrots, scrubbed and cut into ½-inch dice

1 small celery root, peeled and cut into ½-inch dice

3 celery ribs, cut into ½-inch dice

1 leek, white part only, cut into ½-inch dice

3 big garlic cloves, peeled

1 bay leaf

6 baby potatoes

4 oz sorrel, sliced

2½ oz young nettle tips (the top few leaves on each stem)

1¾ oz wild garlic, sliced (flowers kept for garnish)

3 green onions, thinly sliced

Handful of chopped dill

Handful of chopped parsley

Sea salt and black pepper

Crème fraîche, to finish – optional

Towards the end of April and during May, before much grew in people's kitchen gardens, the fields and forests of Ukraine would already be filled with young nettles and wild sorrel. Foraging wasn't so uncommon in the past and is now being rediscovered, in Ukraine and elsewhere.

This nettle, sorrel, and wild garlic soup, which is sometimes called green borsch, can also be made with chicken stock and served with chopped boiled eggs, but usually I just add a spoonful of crème fraîche to my bowl and eat it with a chunk of crusty bread. You don't have to sauté the vegetables before adding the water, but if you do, you will draw out more sweetness from them and the soup will be perfectly balanced: sour, sweet, and slightly hot from the wild garlic and black pepper. If there are any leftovers, you can blitz them to make a puréed soup (which freezes very well) and then serve it with some crumbled blue cheese on top.

Pour the oil into your favorite soup-making pot – I use a cast-iron casserole – and put it over medium-high heat. Once the oil is hot and sizzling, add the onion, carrots, celery root, celery, and leek. Sauté for about 5 minutes, stirring from time to time: you want them to become caramelized in parts, but not scorched. (If the pan feels too crowded, you can fry the vegetables in batches.) Now add the garlic and cook for about 2 minutes, still stirring, until fragrant and starting to get a little color.

Pour in 2½ quarts of cold water and add the bay leaf. Season lightly with salt and bring to a boil, then turn down to a simmer and cook for about 40 minutes with the lid half on.

Add the whole potatoes and cook for 10 minutes, or until they are soft. Finally, add the sorrel, nettle tips, and wild garlic and switch off the heat. Taste the soup and add more salt if needed.

Place a potato in each soup bowl and lightly crush it with a spoon. Ladle the broth over and then sprinkle with the wild garlic flowers, green onions, and herbs to serve. Finish with a dollop of crème fraîche, if you like, and a good grinding of pepper.

Spring lamb broth

SERVES 6

This is a campfire kind of dish, designed for cooking down by the riverside – but with Old Father Thames nearby, instead of the bucolic Dnieper Delta, I make it in my kitchen. It's perfect for the sort of weather where you still need warmth and nourishment, but are ready for fresh flavors. The reason this sort of broth is popular in Ukraine, where it is known as *shurpa*, is thanks to the Tatar community, and versions of it can be found in many countries that were once part of the Ottoman Empire, including Bulgaria and Macedonia; in Romania and the Balkans, it is called *chorpa*.

Normally only garlic and salt would be bashed into a paste and added at the end, but I find that cilantro stalks add an extra layer of flavor and color. Some chickpeas, canned for ease, wouldn't be out of place here either. Simply drain and add them when you add the red bell pepper and chile.

3 lamb shanks
(or lots of lamb bones)

1 large onion, skin on

3 carrots, scrubbed,
2 left whole and 1 sliced

2 celery ribs, roughly chopped

6 baby potatoes

2 tomatoes, grated or chopped

1 large red bell pepper, sliced

1 red chile, bruised

Sea salt and black pepper

CILANTRO PASTE

Handful of cilantro stalks, roughly chopped

2 garlic cloves, roughly chopped

1 tsp sea salt

Place the lamb, onion, whole carrots, and celery in a large saucepan, then pour in 3 quarts of cold water. Season lightly with salt and bring to a boil. Skim off the froth, then turn down the heat to very low and simmer gently for 1½–2 hours, or until the meat is soft and falls off the bone. Make sure the meat stays covered as it cooks: if too much water evaporates, top up the pan with cold water, skimming off any fat that rises to the surface.

Strain the stock into a large bowl, reserving the meat but getting rid of the vegetables – their job is done. Put the meat back into the pan, along with the stock. Now add the sliced carrot and baby potatoes and cook for 10–15 minutes, adding the tomatoes, red bell pepper and chile for the last 2 minutes. Check that the broth is well seasoned.

For the cilantro paste, simply blitz all the ingredients in a food processor, adding a little of the hot broth to help it blend to a smooth paste.

Place a little meat in each soup bowl, then pour the broth over. You can either stir the cilantro paste through the broth or serve it on the side.

Borsch with duck and smoked pears

SERVES 6-8

½ cup beet *kvas* (page 68)
or
¼ cup good-quality red wine vinegar

2 small beets, peeled and cut into thin matchsticks

1 medium onion, finely diced

1 medium carrot, scrubbed and cut into thin matchsticks or coarsely grated

7 oz canned diced tomatoes

10 oz potatoes, peeled and cut into ¾-inch dice

¼ cabbage (anything from green to Savoy), sliced

2 garlic cloves, crushed

Sour cream, to serve

STOCK

2 duck carcasses or 6 duck legs

1 onion, roughly chopped

2 celery ribs, roughly chopped

2 carrots, scrubbed and roughly chopped

Handful of parsley stalks

2 bay leaves

A few sprigs of thyme

4–6 dried smoked pears (page 62) or Agen prunes

Smoked dried fruit is very popular in Ukraine. In Poltava, in central Ukraine, they slowly dry whole pears in the fading heat of a wood-fired oven. What you get is incredible: dried fruit that looks as if it is clad in black leather, with a smoky, complex flavor. There is an adapted method for making these without a wood-fired oven on page 62, so if you happen to find yourself with a glut of pears, why not do a little summer kitchen smoking project of your own? Otherwise, you could just use Agen prunes instead and fry the onion and carrot with some smoked pancetta to add a smoky flavor. You can use any meat stock here – pork is traditional and delicious (try adding blanched and sliced pig's ears for texture, too). But, to me, duck has the most affinity with the depth and richness of the dried fruit.

Pour the beet *kvas* or vinegar over the beets and set aside.

Next make the stock. Put all the stock ingredients except the smoked pears or prunes into a large stockpot and cover with 2½–3 quarts of water. Bring to a boil, skimming off any froth as it appears and, if you are using duck legs, season lightly with salt – this way the meat will be properly seasoned. Add the smoked pears or prunes and simmer for 1–1½ hours over low heat – if using duck legs, the meat should be falling off the bones.

When the stock has been simmering for about an hour, use a ladle to skim some of the fat from the stock and put it into a frying pan over medium heat. Add the onion and cook until soft and taking on some color, then add the carrot and cook until the vegetables start caramelizing – keep skimming and adding fat if the pan seems dry. Now add the beets, together with the liquid they have been pickling in, and cook for 2 minutes, then add the tomatoes and cook over high heat for another 3 minutes. Take off the heat.

Strain the duck stock into another saucepan, returning the smoked pears or prunes to the stock. Discard (or compost) the vegetables – and the duck carcasses, if that's what you used. If you used duck legs, take the meat off the bones and put it in with the stock as well.

Now add the contents of the frying pan to the stock and bring to a boil. Add the potatoes and simmer for 5 minutes, then add the cabbage and cook for another 5 minutes. Stir in the crushed garlic at the very end, when you are ready to switch off the heat.

Ladle into soup bowls and serve with a spoonful of sour cream.

БОРЩ З КАЧКОЮ І КОПЧЕНИМИ ГРУШАМИ

Split pea and bread soup

SERVES 6

½ lb yellow or green split peas, soaked overnight

½ small celery root

1 parsnip, peeled

1 carrot, scrubbed

1 celery rib

1 onion, peeled

4 garlic cloves, peeled

3 Tbsp canola oil

2 Tbsp tomato paste

3 sprigs of thyme, leaves only

4 oz stale sourdough or good rye bread, cut into chunks

Sea salt and black pepper

Olive oil, chopped marjoram or oregano, and chile flakes, to serve

Called *kuleshnyk* in Ukraine, this soup is somewhere between a minestrone and *ribollita* in its nature. My vegetarian husband, Joe, tells me that this recipe – adapted from Zinovia Klynovetska's 1913 *Dishes and Drinks of Ukraine* – is his favorite in this whole book. Dried leftover bread is used to thicken the soup, adding comfort too. A slick of olive oil over the *kuleshnyk* when served, a rather Italian maneuver, works very well here.

Drain the split peas in a colander and rinse them under cold running water.

Peel the skin off the celery root with a knife, being sure to cut away all the bits that harbor soil in them. Dice the celery root finely but not necessarily perfectly – chopping it finely will draw out more flavor as it cooks, but this is still a rustic dish, so don't worry about being too precise. Do the same with the parsnip, carrot, celery, onion, and garlic.

Heat the oil in a stockpot or large saucepan over medium heat. Add the onion and cook until the onion softens and starts to color. Next add all the other vegetables except the garlic and cook, stirring from time to time, for 15–20 minutes, or until they are golden all over. If the pan looks dry at any point, add a splash of water and scrape the bottom of the pan with a wooden spoon. Now add the garlic and tomato paste and get a little color on the garlic too, then add the thyme. Do take your time with browning the vegetables, as this is where most of the flavor will come from.

When the vegetables look brown and softened, add 2 quarts of cold water and a generous pinch of salt. Bring to a boil, then turn down the heat and simmer for 15 minutes. Add the split peas and cook for 30 minutes, or until they are soft. Finally, add the bread and cook for 5 more minutes.

Taste and adjust the seasoning, then ladle into soup bowls. I like serving this with a slick of olive oil, a little bit of my beloved marjoram, and a pinch of chile flakes.

Southern borsch with a giant dumpling

SERVES 6

---

1 whole organic chicken or cockerel, about 2½ lb

2 onions, peeled, 1 halved and 1 finely diced

2 bay leaves

5 oz (¾ cup) dried borlotti beans, soaked overnight (or 7 oz/1 cup drained canned borlotti beans)

2 potatoes, peeled and cut into 1¼-inch chunks

1 large carrot, scrubbed and coarsely grated

2 pink or red beets, peeled and cut into thin matchsticks

1 red bell pepper, thinly sliced

14.5 oz canned diced tomatoes (or fresh, if in season)

½ small green or Savoy cabbage, thinly sliced

Handful of chopped dill

1-2 garlic cloves, roughly chopped

Sea salt and black pepper

Crème fraîche and dill fronds, to serve

DUMPLING

⅓ cup kefir

¾ cup (100g) all-purpose flour

Scant ½ tsp baking soda

This type of borsch is very local to where I grew up in the south of Ukraine. Borsch is made with *galushky* (small dumplings) in other parts of Ukraine, but nowhere else have I encountered a recipe with a loaf-like dumpling that you take out and slice, and I am proud to record it in this book. Sometimes they would even go as far as stuffing the dumpling inside the cockerel! Traditionally, nothing but meat and onions go into the stock, but do flavor it with other vegetables or aromatics if you wish.

Put the chicken or cockerel, the halved onion, and the bay leaves into a large stockpot with 5 quarts of cold water. Salt lightly and bring to a boil, then turn down the heat as low as it will go and skim off any foam from the surface. Cook for about 45 minutes, then check if the chicken is done by pulling at the leg: it should come away from the carcass easily.

If using dried borlotti beans, drain and cook in a saucepan of boiling water for 45 minutes–1 hour or until soft.

Strain the stock and return to the pot, along with the bird; discard (or compost) the onion and bay leaves. Add the potatoes to the pot and boil for about 7 minutes.

Meanwhile, use a ladle to skim some fat from the stock and put it into a large frying pan over medium-low heat. When it sizzles, add the diced onion and cook, stirring, until the onion softens, then add the carrot and cook for another 5 minutes. If it seems dry at any point, skim a little more fat off the stock and add to the pan. You are looking to slightly caramelize the onion and carrot, to draw out the sugars. Add the beets and red bell pepper and cook for 2 minutes before stirring in the tomatoes. Boil rapidly for a few minutes, then tip the contents of the frying pan into the pot, along with the cabbage and drained beans. Simmer for 3-4 minutes. Taste the soup: it should be sour, sweet, and well seasoned.

To make the dumpling, put the kefir into a bowl with a good pinch of salt. Sift in the flour with the baking soda and use your hands to bring everything together. Tip out onto a flour-dusted surface and knead until you have a very light, soft dough – it shouldn't be sticky, so sprinkle over and knead in more flour if needed. Shape into a large dumpling, then carefully lower into the soup and simmer gently for 25 minutes.

Use a mortar and pestle to bash the chopped dill to a paste with the garlic, adding a splash of the hot borsch or oil to loosen to a sauce consistency. Lift the chicken and dumpling out of the borsch and onto a serving plate, then cut the dumpling into slices and drizzle with the dill and garlic sauce. Ladle the borsch into bowls and serve with crème fraîche and a few fronds of dill.

Fish broth with dill and garlic *lyok*

SERVES 6-8 IN THE WILD

Originally a campfire soup for cooking freshly caught fish on a riverbank, this broth is common in many regions, especially Besarabia and my home region of Kherson. Any smaller fish from the day's catch, like gobies, would be used for the stock and then discarded, while the bigger fish would be chopped, poached, and served with the broth.

I once made this for 300 academics at the Oxford Symposium of Food, using sea bass heads. Most people smiled and tucked in with fervor, but I think some were rather taken aback! I hope you won't be: together with the pleasantly chewy millet, the fish heads make for a simple but outstanding broth. Good-sized fish heads hold quite a lot of tasty flesh too, and most local fishmongers will give you them for free. Alternatively, you could buy four whole fish and ask for them to be filleted, keeping the heads, tails, and bones. Save the fillets for another meal, or if you're making this for a dinner party, panfry them and serve them with the broth. The finished broth is further fortified by a dill, garlic, and salt paste called *lyok* (or *salamur* in the southwest of Ukraine).

7 oz celery root, peeled and cubed

2 carrots, scrubbed and roughly chopped

2 onions, unpeeled, halved

2 celery ribs, roughly chopped

2 bay leaves

4 fish heads and tails – plus the bones, if possible (I used bream, but any sustainable white fish would be fine)

½ cup millet

3½ Tbsp butter

1 large juicy tomato (or a couple of smaller ones)

LYOK

2 large garlic cloves, peeled

1 tsp sea salt

½ cup dill, roughly chopped

1 red or green chile, seeded and roughly chopped

Put the celery root, carrots, onions, celery, and bay leaves into a large stockpot and cover with 2½ quarts of cold water. Bring to a boil, then lower the heat and simmer for 20 minutes.

Strain the stock, discarding (or composting) the vegetables, and return the stock to the stockpot. Add the cleaned fish heads and tails – and the bones, if using – and cook over low heat for 15 minutes. Now add the millet and simmer for 15 minutes, or until cooked. Fish out and discard the bones, if you used them.

Heat the butter in a frying pan over medium heat, grate in the tomato, discarding the skins, and cook for 5 minutes or so, then add to the broth.

To make the *lyok*, blitz the garlic, salt, dill, and chile to a paste in a blender or food processor. Swoosh in ½ cup of the hot fish broth to loosen it up and tame the raw garlic flavor. Blitz briefly to combine, then transfer to a small bowl.

Ladle the broth into soup bowls and place a fish head or tail in each one. Serve with a small spoonful of *lyok* and some more chopped dill.

Chicken broth with bran *kvas*, noodles, mushrooms, and lovage

SERVES 6

3 small onions, peeled

3 carrots, scrubbed

2 celery ribs, chopped

¼ celery root, peeled and chopped

1 x 2½-lb organic or free-range chicken, jointed

1 bay leaf, crumbled or torn

2 Tbsp butter

2 Tbsp canola or olive oil

8 oz wild or cremini mushrooms, sliced

1 cup wheat bran and polenta *kvas* (page 67) or pickle or sauerkraut juice

1 cup lovage or celery leaves, chopped

Crème fraîche, to serve – optional

NOODLES

2 eggs

1⅔ cups (200g) all-purpose flour or 1½ cups (200g) '00' pasta flour

If you don't fancy making your own noodles for this, feel free to use good-quality Asian egg noodles. On the other hand, you could make an extra batch of noodles and dry them – they'll keep in an airtight container for a few weeks, ready for your next broth... The flavor of proper *zama* (or *zeama*, as this soup is called closer to the Moldovan border) comes from bran *kvas* and lovage. If lovage is hard to find, use celery leaves instead – the flavor is close enough. Equally, while I recommend trying your hand at making bran *kvas* (it's not difficult!), if you don't have any, add a splash of any ferment brine that is easy to get – sauerkraut or pickle juice works well – or even just a squeeze of lemon juice.

Roughly chop half the onions and half the carrots, then pop into a large stockpot. Add the celery, celery root, chicken, bay leaf, and 2 quarts of cold water. Bring to a boil, skim off any froth from the surface, then simmer for about 1 hour, until the chicken is tender and the meat is falling off the bones.

Meanwhile, make the noodles. Put the eggs into a bowl and beat lightly. Gradually add the flour, mixing with a spoon at first, then bringing the dough together with your hands. Knead until you have a smooth, tight dough. Cover with a clean kitchen towel or plastic wrap and leave to rest for at least 15 minutes, or up to 1 hour.

If the dough feels dry and leathery, do not dust your bench with flour, but if the dough feels tacky, give the bench a generous dusting. Cut the dough in half and roll out each half with a rolling pin into a 12-inch square sheet about 1/16 inch thick. Dust the sheets well with flour, then roll up into sausage shapes and thinly slice. Gently unravel the noodles and leave to dry on a clean towel.

Dice the rest of the onions and grate the remaining carrots. Heat half the butter and half the oil in a frying pan over medium-low heat. When it sizzles, add the onions and soften for a few minutes, then add the carrots and cook until starting to caramelize – this will add natural sweetness to the broth. Tip into the stockpot.

Heat the rest of the butter and oil in the same frying pan over medium-high heat and fry the mushrooms until golden, then add them to the stockpot as well. Finally, add the *kvas* or brine and the lovage or celery to the broth and simmer for 2 minutes.

Boil the noodles in a pan of salted boiling water for about a minute, until just cooked, then drain, keeping them moistened with a little of the broth. (You can cook the noodles directly in the broth, if you like, but it will make it thicker and cloudy.) Put some noodles and chicken into each soup bowl, then ladle over the broth and serve with a spoonful of crème fraîche, if you like.

Tripe soup

SERVES 8

---

1 lb raw or dressed tripe

5 allspice berries

5 black peppercorns

2 bay leaves

2 small onions, peeled, 1 left whole and 1 finely diced

2 carrots, 1 roughly chopped, 1 cut into thin matchsticks

2 celery ribs, 1 roughly chopped, 1 finely diced

2 Tbsp butter

2 Tbsp vegetable oil

2 Tbsp tomato paste

2 Tbsp all-purpose flour

1–2 tsp smoked and/or hot paprika

½ cup white wine

1 quart chicken stock or water

¼–½ cup cream

1 garlic clove, finely chopped

A little bit of grated nutmeg

Sea salt and black pepper

Marjoram (or oregano) and lovage leaves, to serve

CROUTONS

A few slices of stale rye bread

Olive or canola oil

Good pinch of chile flakes

I know offal makes some people uneasy, but there is no need to be alarmed when it comes to tripe. Clean tripe smells like fresh milk, and I adore its velvety, slightly crunchy texture – if you are a meat eater, I implore you to give it a go. Actually, I wonder if the word "tripe" is partly responsible for its bad reputation? After all, tripe rhymes with gripe. In the Polish-influenced cuisine of Halychyna, in western Ukraine, tripe is usually cooked in a soup like this one, and its name is the much more endearing *flyachky*.

Recently I have been making ridiculous amounts of sourdough. In the absence of hungry chickens, it feels criminal to throw away stale bread, so I use it to make croutons for soups like this one.

If using raw tripe, put it in a saucepan and cover with cold water. Bring to a boil and drain. Repeat this three times until your tripe smells more like milk than anything compromising.

Wrap the allspice, peppercorns, and bay leaves in cheesecloth, tying the top securely. Put into a saucepan, along with the tripe, and cover with cold water. Add the whole onion and the roughly chopped carrot and celery and simmer for 1–2 hours – the tripe is done when it is tender but still a little crunchy. Drain, discarding the liquid, vegetables, and aromatics, then cut the tripe into ½-inch strips.

While the tripe is cooking, make the croutons. Preheat the oven to 400°F. Cut the bread into cubes and scatter over a baking sheet, then drizzle with oil and sprinkle with sea salt and chile flakes and bake until golden and crisp. These will keep in an airtight container for months.

Heat the butter and oil in a heavy-based casserole over medium-low heat. Add the diced onion and celery and cook for about 5 minutes, stirring every so often, until the onion is translucent and just starting to color. Add the tomato paste, flour, and paprika and cook, stirring constantly, for 2 minutes.

Pour in the wine and cook for a minute, scraping the base of the pan to deglaze and stirring so the flour doesn't form clumps. Now add the stock or water, carrot matchsticks, and tripe strips and cook for 20 minutes. Whisk in the cream, garlic, and nutmeg and season really well with salt and pepper.

Let the soup rest, covered with a lid, for 5 minutes or so, then ladle into soup bowls and scatter over some croutons and herb leaves.

Mushroom broth with sour pickles

SERVES 4

4 oz dried porcini or wild mushrooms

2 quarts hot water

¼ cup pearl barley (or rice or buckwheat)

2 onions, peeled, 1 left whole and 1 finely diced

10 oz potatoes, peeled and cut into ¾-inch dice

5 oz quick-fermented cucumbers (page 26) or jarred pickles

2 Tbsp butter

1 Tbsp vegetable oil

1 carrot, scrubbed and coarsely grated

1 parsnip, peeled and coarsely grated

¼ small celery root, peeled and coarsely grated

2 garlic cloves, finely chopped

1¼–2 cups brine from the quick-fermented cucumbers or pickle juice from the jar

Sea salt and black pepper

Rye bread, marjoram or oregano leaves and crème fraîche, to serve – optional

This soup was inspired by a Ukrainian food writer called Marianna Dushar. A generous and sensitive cook, she taught me all about the culinary specialities of Halychyna, a historic and geographical region around Lviv, in western Ukraine.

In most of Ukraine, this is better known as a meat-heavy broth, made with pork or beef ribs, although my mum often used duck – any meat that benefits from the sharpness of a pickle juice works well. However, I longed to cook a similar broth for my vegetarian friends and husband, so when I came across Marianna's version, using root vegetables and mushrooms, I was over the moon.

Soak the dried mushrooms in the hot water for 30 minutes.

Meanwhile, cook the barley in salted boiling water for about 20–30 minutes, or until nice and soft. Drain and set aside. (If using rice or buckwheat, they'll only need 10–15 minutes.)

Drain the mushrooms, reserving the liquid but leaving behind any sandy residue, then finely chop the mushrooms. Pour the mushroom liquid into a stockpot and add the mushrooms and the whole onion. Season lightly with salt and pepper, then cook for 10 minutes. Now add the potatoes and cook for 15 minutes or until tender.

While the potatoes are cooking, slice half the cucumbers or pickles into circles and grate the other half on the coarse side of a box grater.

Heat the butter and oil in a frying pan over medium heat. Add the diced onion and cook until transparent and softened. Now add the grated carrot, parsnip, and celery root and cook for about 5 minutes, stirring often. If the pan looks a bit dry at any point, add a little more butter or a splash of water. Add the garlic and cook for another 2 minutes. Finally, stir in all the cucumbers or pickles, both sliced and grated, and the brine. Let it simmer for a minute.

Now tip the contents of the frying pan into the stockpot, along with the barley (or rice or buckwheat). Bring to a boil, just to warm everything through, then take off the heat. Fish out the whole onion and discard (or compost).

Ladle into soup bowls and serve with rye bread, some marjoram or oregano, and some crème fraîche, if you fancy it.

Bread, pasta, and dumplings

THE ALCHEMY OF FLOUR AND WATER

In Ukraine, people regularly used to make bread without commercial yeast. My Aunt Lyuda, for example, just lets mashed potato go sour overnight, then uses this to help leaven her traditional Easter bread, or _paskha_.

Hops were also traditionally used as a source of wild yeasts. Hop crowns would be steeped in hot water to draw out the yeasts that cling to the droopy hop clusters, then the cooled yeast-rich water would be mixed with flour and left to ferment. Or pounded hop flowers, flour, and a little water would be mixed into a mush, rolled into small pellets, and dried in the sun. These dried pellets are still sold at the local market in my hometown of Kakhovka by a woman called Lilya, who looks like she is in her nineties, and I worry about how much longer there will be vendors and buyers for this sort of thing.

In Besarabia, in the southwest of Ukraine, they use hard discs called _turta_ ("torte") for making a sourdough starter. Consisting of corn flour mixed with grape must or pomace and then dried, these are reconstituted in water and left to ferment into a starter, with the lively yeasts from the grape skins helping the process along. And in the mountains of western Ukraine, Hutsul women used to pinch off a little bit of their sourdough before it was shaped and baked, and bury it deep inside a sack of rye flour. Encased in the flour, it would keep until the next time they needed to make bread, when it would be rehydrated and the breadmaking cycle repeated.

The recipe for traditional Ukrainian bread that follows has a straightforward method for making your own starter – but if you want to make things easier, ask a friend or a friendly sourdough bakery for 6 tablespoons of their starter. Then you'll be ready to make your own dark rye and sourdough breads. I realize that such traditionally made breads take time and may not have the mass appeal of bread made with commercial yeast, but I am keen to bring back the culture that existed in pre-Soviet Ukraine, and before modern manufacturing in general, with its industrialized, denatured, and overrefined food.

Pasta and dumplings both begin with a simple dough; it's hard to beat a comforting bowl of homemade pasta with a nutty, buttery sauce. The dumpling dough on page 174 is universal, so with that in your repertoire, you can easily turn your hand to all kinds of dumplings – the essay on _varenyky_, at the end of the chapter, has plenty of ideas and inspiration to get you started. Whatever else you try, I would also urge you to have a go at making the good-for-you spelt dumplings filled with kraut (page 172). They are very filling and nutritious, and in my family we can't get enough of them, especially in the colder months of the year.

"The flat brown cake of Ukrainian bread"

MAKES 1 LOAF

One of my favorite writers, John Steinbeck, was perceived by the Soviet authorities to be a communist sympathizer of sorts. For this reason they allowed him and Magnum photographer Robert Capa to visit the USSR in 1947. They traveled through Russia, Ukraine, and Georgia – and Steinbeck's warm words and Capa's photographs from this trip are my all-time favorite account of traveling in Ukraine. Steinbeck seemed to really enjoy the place and its people: "They were laughing people… There was an openness and a heartiness about them." I love his observations of peasant life and the descriptions of the outlandish feasts they were served. He also mentions the ubiquitous dark rye bread more than once, writing, "That fireplace and oven is raised about four feet above the floor, and in this the bread is baked, the flat brown cakes of Ukrainian bread, which are very good."

It is true that the dark, dense rye bread we call "black bread" is part of the Ukrainian identity. There isn't any bread I enjoy more than this one. It is the quintessential Ukrainian loaf, with deep flavor and sweetness from molasses – the sort of bread that needs nothing more than butter or a sliver of *salo* (cured pork fat) or smoked salmon, perhaps a shot of ice-cold vodka, and some pickles.

RYE STARTER

5⅔ cups (580g) organic whole-grain rye flour, plus extra for feeding

2½ cups tepid non-chlorinated water, plus extra for feeding

>>

For the starter, mix 6 tablespoons of the flour and 3 tablespoons of the water in a 16-ounce jar with a lid, cover with a clean kitchen towel or plastic wrap, and put in a warm, dark place for 1–3 days, depending on the temperature. When ready for the next stage, it will be slightly bubbly and should smell pleasant – like flour, not yet funky or sour. Add another 6 tablespoons of flour and another 3 tablespoons of tepid water to the jar and mix well. Put it back in a warm, dark place for another day – it should increase in volume by almost half and become bubblier.

Finally add ¾ cup of flour and 6 tablespoons of tepid water and in under a day it will rise and become properly bubbly. There – you are done, put the lid on the jar and transfer your starter to the fridge. For the next week, get rid of roughly half the starter every morning, then add ½ cup of flour and ¼ cup of tepid water. By the end of the week, your starter should be very stable.

From now on, to feed your starter, remove ¼ cup of it every other day if you can (but if you forget about it, it should be fine for a week) and use it to make bread, or gift it, or chuck it, then add ¼ cup of flour and 2 tablespoons of tepid water back into the jar.

>>

BREAD

¾ cup (180g) activated rye
starter (see page 150)

1½ cups tepid water

2 Tbsp molasses
or
3 Tbsp soft dark brown sugar

2½ tsp fine sea salt

4¾ cups (500g) organic
whole-grain rye flour

2 tsp caraway seeds

2 tsp coriander seeds

When you want to bake bread, take ¼ cup of starter from the jar and activate it by adding ½ cup of flour and ¼ cup of tepid water, then leaving it for 6–11 hours. Now it is ready to use.

The day before you want to bake the bread, whisk the starter with the tepid water in a large bowl until frothy, then add the molasses or sugar and salt and whisk again. Gradually add the flour, using wet hands to mix the dough in the bowl – it will be frustratingly sticky, but don't worry, just bring it together the best you can. Cover the bowl with plastic wrap and leave at room temperature overnight, if it's winter; in the summer, put it in the fridge.

The next day, line a baking sheet with baking parchment. The dough will look more together, if not much risen. Wet your hands really well and pick up the dough from the bowl, then flatten it into a disc shape and tuck the edges under, shaping it into a ball. The dough will still feel tacky, but have faith! Put the dough ball onto the baking sheet, wet your hands again, and stroke the bread, smoothing the top, then cover with plastic wrap and leave somewhere warm for 2 hours.

After the bread has been proofing for about an hour, the dough will spread out. My kitchen is often very cold in winter, so at this point I sometimes put mine on a rack on top of the stove if I have the oven on. During the summer, I just leave it on a sunny windowsill. In the remaining hour of the proofing time, the dough will rise ever so slightly.

Preheat the oven to 475°F.

Uncover your bread and spray or brush it with water, then sprinkle the caraway and coriander seeds over the top.

Bake the bread, still on its baking sheet, for 20 minutes, then lower the oven temperature to 400°F and bake for another 30 minutes.

Take it out and peel off the baking parchment, then let it cool completely on a wire rack. Do not be tempted to cut the bread while it's warm. It's actually recommended to cut rye bread the next day, but I never manage to wait that long! The bread will look suspiciously flat, but that's the beauty of it, as the crust – which you will have a lot of – tastes ambrosial.

Sourdough (for beginners)

MAKES 1 LOAF

When I first met Katrya Kalyuzhna, I had been wanting to make sourdough bread for years. Katrya had started a micro-bakery in her house in Kakhovka and had given my mum a little bit of her starter and taught her the method she used. Well, soon my mum was completely obsessed, and within a couple of months she got really good at making sourdough. I gave her a bunch of cookbooks, including Chad Robertson's *Tartine Bread* and Richard Bertinet's *Dough*, and she took a little bit from everywhere and came up with this method.

Encouraged by my mum's success, I asked her to bring some of her starter to the UK and I watched her make bread a few times, jotting down notes on a piece of paper. When she went back to Ukraine, I rolled up my sleeves and made a successful sourdough loaf – my first ever! This is sourdough for beginners, and it worked (and still works) for me, a busy mum living in the city. I bake it once a week and normally start on a Friday, knowing that I'll be around the following day. You won't have to do much the next day, by the way – just be at home or nearby.

Sourdough bread keeps well and is excellent sliced, frozen, and then revived in a toaster. And the good news is that a sourdough starter is more robust than you might think: unless it turns pink and smells rancid, which would take at least a good few months of total abandonment, it can be rescued (see below).

SOURDOUGH STARTER

Rye starter (page 150) or other sourdough starter

⅓ cup (40g) bread flour

3 Tbsp tepid non-chlorinated water, plus more for feeding

All-purpose and/or whole-grain flour, for feeding

>>

You can either use some rye starter or any sourdough starter that has been given to you – it does not have to be rye. Remove the starter from the fridge, take out 3 tablespoons, and mix it with the bread flour and tepid water, then leave it, covered with a clean kitchen towel or plastic wrap, for about 6 hours at room temperature, until bubbles appear. Your starter is now activated and ready to use.

To feed the remainder of your starter in the jar, add 3 tablespoons of all-purpose and/or whole-grain flour and 1½ tablespoons of tepid water. Leave it with the lid half-open for 3–6 hours at room temperature, then back into the fridge it goes. Basically, whatever you take out of the jar needs to be replenished by the same weight of 1:1 of starter and water. That's it! (Next time you want to use your starter, if you realize you have forgotten about it and you see liquid on top, do not panic. Strain off the liquid, remove 3 tablespoons of starter, and feed the remaining starter in the jar with 3 tablespoons of all-purpose and/or whole-grain flour and 1½ tablespoons of tepid water.)

>>

½ cup (120g) activated sourdough starter (see page 154)

1½ cups tepid water

2½ cups (300g) organic whole-grain flour

1⅔ cups (200g) organic bread flour

1 Tbsp fine sea salt

Fine semolina or polenta, for sprinkling

Sesame seeds, for sprinkling – optional

Plop your bubbly activated starter into a large bowl with the tepid water (bits of starter floating on top are a sign that the starter is ready) and whisk until frothy and homogenous. Gradually add both the flours, folding them in with a spatula to make a rough-looking mixture. Cover the bowl with plastic wrap or a clean kitchen towel and leave at room temperature for 1 hour. During this time, a process called autolysis occurs, bringing the dough together.

Next you need to incorporate the salt. Sprinkle in a little of the salt, wet your hands, and pat the dough where you've sprinkled the salt. Grasp one side of the dough in your fingers, pull it up and fold it over the salt. Repeat this action again and again, rotating the bowl 90 degrees every time, and adding the remaining salt until all of it is incorporated. Cover and leave at room temperature for 1 hour.

Now start stretching and folding the dough in its bowl. To do this, pinch one side of the dough between your fingers and stretch it up as far as it will go without tearing, then fold it over. Rotate the dough, then stretch the side up and fold it over again. Do this four times, then cover the bowl with a kitchen towel and leave for 30 minutes. Repeat this process two more times, each time giving the dough a 30-minute break in-between.

Line a large bowl or proofing basket with baking parchment, allowing plenty of overhang, and sprinkle with a little semolina or polenta.

To shape the dough, on a lightly floured surface, slightly flatten it into a rough rectangle. Place it on your worktop with one of the shorter sides nearest to you. Lift up the bottom right-hand corner of the dough and fold it into the center, then lift up the bottom left-hand corner of the dough and fold that into the center too. Move your hands a bit further up the rectangle and grasp the edge of the dough on each side between your fingers, then fold first the right side and then the left side into the center. Repeat this two more times, each time moving your hands further up the dough. Now roll up the dough, starting from the end nearest to you, and flip it, seam side down, into the lined bowl or proofing basket. Cover with plastic wrap and leave in the fridge overnight.

The next day, take the bowl or basket of dough out of the fridge and leave at room temperature for an hour or longer. The dough needs to lose the chill of the fridge and come alive again, and in winter this might take several hours.

Preheat your oven to its highest setting, with a heavy-based cast-iron pot and its lid in there – the idea is to heat it to the max.

Once your pot has been in the oven for at least 30 minutes, put the bowl with the bread near the oven. Sprinkle the loaf with a little flour, semolina, or polenta for extra texture and scatter with the sesame seeds, if using. If you have a lame, use it to slash the top, but if you forget it is not the end of the world.

You have to work quickly now, being careful not to burn yourself, as the pot will be extremely hot. Using oven mitts, take the pot out of the oven (leave the oven door open) and take off the lid. Gently, but surely, grab hold of the baking parchment with your bread on it and lower it inside the pot. With your oven mitts on, put the lid back on the pot and carefully slide it onto the middle rack of the oven.

Bake the bread for 30 minutes, then take off the lid and lower the oven temperature to 425°F. After 20 minutes, put on your oven mitts and remove the pot from the oven, then immediately lift out the bread (I hold on to the baking parchment and use a thin spatula to help prize it out). Peel off the baking parchment – don't stress if some of it has stuck to the bottom, it will peel off more easily later – then leave the loaf on a wire rack, resisting the temptation to cut into it before it has completely cooled.

Sourdough garlic buns

SERVES 5
(MAKES 10 BUNS)

¼ cup (60g) sourdough starter (page 154)

1 cup whole milk

2½ cups (300g) all-purpose flour

3 eggs

⅓ cup (60g) superfine sugar

1⅔ cups (200g) bread flour

2 tsp fine sea salt

3½ Tbsp (50g) unsalted butter, softened

1 beaten egg, to glaze

TO SERVE

2 garlic cloves, roughly chopped

3 Tbsp roughly chopped dill

Pinch of flaky sea salt

1½ Tbsp canola or unrefined sunflower oil

So many Eastern European dishes have similar names and renditions, but these buns, called *pampushky*, are undeniably Ukrainian; no other country ever claims them. They are doused in garlic oil as soon as they come out of the oven, and the smell of freshly baked, slightly sweet buns mingled with strong garlic makes my head spin. Traditionally served with borsch (page 132), they are also excellent with any broth or just eaten with a sliver of *salo* (cured pork fat) and a pickle.

The day before you want to bake the buns (or 2 days before, if you plan to proof the dough overnight), make your starter sponge. Whisk the starter into ¼ cup of the milk until it has dissolved, then add ¾ cup (100g) of the all-purpose flour and mix well. Cover with plastic wrap and leave in the fridge overnight. (If you don't have a sourdough starter, you can make these buns with the yeasted dough on page 300.)

Next day, the starter sponge should be smoother and slightly bigger. Fit an electric mixer with the whisk attachment and, with the machine running, pinch off pieces of the sponge and drop into the mixer bowl. When all the sponge is in the bowl, whisk in the eggs, sugar, and the remaining milk. Stir in the bread flour and the rest of the all-purpose flour and briefly mix to a rough dough. Cover the bowl with plastic wrap and leave for an hour or so to let the dough come together.

Grease a large bowl with butter. Add the salt and butter to the dough and mix for about 5 minutes, until it becomes very stretchy. Scoop the dough into the buttered bowl. Cover the bowl and leave it either somewhere warm for about 6 hours, or in the fridge overnight. When it's ready, the dough should have doubled in size. If you proofed the dough in the fridge, transfer it to another bowl and leave it at room temperature for about an hour – it needs to wake up and lose the chill of the fridge.

Grease a rectangular baking pan about 8 inches long and 2½ inches deep with a little butter or oil. Turn out the dough onto a floured surface and give it a quick knead until it stops sticking to your hands. With floured hands, divide the dough into ten 4-ounce pieces and shape into smooth balls. Place the balls snugly in the pan, arranging them in two rows. Cover with plastic wrap and leave somewhere warm for about 1–2 hours – they will merge and double in size as they proof.

Preheat the oven to 425°F. Gently brush the buns with egg glaze and bake for 50 minutes – if they start to look too dark on top, cover with foil. Use a mortar and pestle to crush the garlic and dill to a paste with the salt, then whisk in the oil. Drizzle over the buns once they are out of the oven.

Ukrainian wedding bread

MAKES 1 LOAF

Like a lot of Slavic food culture, *korovai* has pagan history. The etymological origins of the word are contested, but most theories trace it to *korova* (cow), a symbol of fertility and well-being. The bread, wrapped in an embroidered cloth called *rushnyk*, would be presented to the bride and groom just before they got married. Normally a really huge *korovai* would be baked. Seven women, including the bride, would partake in making it, and traditionally older women, happy in their marriage, would be called in to help. Songs would be sung while the *korovai* was kneaded, the women's wisdom and positive energy seeping into the rich, sweet dough with every push of their palms. The decorations, made out of flour, water, and salt, related to nature – doves, leaves, flowers, heads of wheat, sun, moon, and stars – and these would be kept as souvenirs for many years after the wedding.

The breads you see in this picture were made by the legendary Kateryna Porskalo, who lives in Opishnya, near Poltava, and has been making *korovai* in her wood-fired *pich* at home for 36 years. She also makes *medyanyky* – small honey breads made out of a similar dough. She is so expert and well-known that someone once phoned her from New York to order a *korovai*, which she duly baked and sent in a van to Kyiv. They flew to Kyiv to pick up the *korovai* and took it back on the plane with them to New York.

Don't panic, though, I will not make you do the 25-pound beauty you see on the right. I think starting with the smaller one may be wiser if this is your first time – you can always increase the quantities once you've practiced this version. You'll need a 10½-inch round cake pan, ideally about 4 inches deep.

1 x ¼-oz packet fast-action dried yeast

1 cup whey or buttermilk

¾ cup (150g) superfine sugar

5¾ cups (700g) all-purpose flour

4 eggs

1 Tbsp fine sea salt

¼ cup (60g) unsalted butter

3½ Tbsp (50g) lard

¼ cup yogurt

2 tsp vanilla extract

1 Tbsp anise seeds – optional

>>

Put the yeast into the bowl of an electric mixer and mix in the whey or buttermilk and ¼ cup (50g) of the sugar. Whisk in 1¼ cups (150g) of the flour, then cover the bowl and leave for about 1 hour, or until bubbles appear on the surface. Add the eggs and the salt, along with the rest of the sugar and flour, and mix well. At this point I normally stick it all into an electric mixer fitted with the dough hook and mix to bring everything together. When you have a smooth dough, cover the bowl and leave somewhere warm for an hour to proof.

Now add the butter, lard, yogurt, vanilla extract, and anise seeds, if using, and mix well with the dough hook. The dough will become sticky and wet, but don't worry. Cover again and leave somewhere warm for another hour.

>>

GLAZE

1 egg, lightly beaten

DECORATIONS

1⅔ cups (200g) all-purpose flour

7 Tbsp (100g) fine sea salt

1 egg, lightly beaten

By this point the dough should look lively and light, but it will still be sticky. Now this is where the fun begins: flour your worktop really well and knead the bread. Keep kneading until the dough stops sticking to your hands – it should still feel very soft. Shape it into a large ball by tucking the sides underneath and feeling the top stretch and tighten.

Butter a 10½-inch round deep cake pan. Put the dough into the pan, cover with a clean kitchen towel, and leave to rise somewhere warm for 2 hours, or until almost doubled in size.

Preheat the oven to 400°F. Gently brush the egg glaze over the top of the bread and bake for 1 hour and 20 minutes. Keep an eye on it, and if the top starts becoming too dark, cover with foil. When the bread is cooked, remove from the oven and cool on a wire rack.

Meanwhile, make the "dead dough" for the decorations. Pour ½ cup of water into a bowl, then whisk in the flour and salt. Bring together to make a dough, then turn out onto a flour-dusted surface and knead well – the dough should be fairly tight. Cover and leave to rest for at least 15 minutes.

When it comes to shaping the decorations, you can make beautifully simple leaves and flowers, like those on Kateryna's breads. Or you can settle down at the kitchen table on a rainy afternoon and put on the radio. Google "pagan sun and moon designs" or "salt dough roses tutorial," or base your designs on the kind of flowers that adorn Ukrainian flower beds, such as periwinkles, marigolds, and poppies. That's exactly what I did, as you can see in the photo here.

Line a baking sheet with baking parchment, then place your decorations on it and bake at 400°F for 10–15 minutes, or until they firm up. Glaze with the beaten egg and bake for another 10–15 minutes, or until golden. Cool on a wire rack. (If not using right away, keep the decorations in an airtight container – otherwise they will go soft and pale.)

The best way to attach your decorations to the bread is by using toothpicks: carefully insert one end into the decoration and then press down into the bread where you want it to go. Note that the decorations themselves are not edible – and take care to remove the toothpicks before eating the bread!

Yeasted buns with slow-roast pork

SERVES 5
(MAKES 10 BUNS)

1 x ¼-oz packet fast-action dried yeast

½ cup lukewarm whole milk

¼ cup (50g) superfine sugar

3½ Tbsp unsalted butter, softened

2 egg yolks

½ tsp vanilla extract

1 tsp fine sea salt

2 cups (250g) all-purpose flour

About 1 lb leftover slow-roast pork with kraut and dried fruit (page 262), chopped

1 egg, beaten

If you are a meat eater, there are two recipes you simply must cook from this book: the slow-roast pork with kraut and dried fruit; and these buns, conveniently filled with some of the leftover pork (or duck confit if all the pork has disappeared!), chopped and stirred through the kraut and fruit. This happy combination came about one year when my mother was making her usual sweet *pyrizhky* buns for Christmas, filled with curd cheese and raisins, but thought she would try stuffing them with this savory filling instead. When I tasted them, I nearly fell off my chair: rich sweet dough and a sweet, slightly sour filling, with the odd piece of tender pork among the juicy prunes and apricots.

Do not be scared to add the vanilla to the dough: it works! You can also make the buns with a variety of sweet fillings, such as poppyseed paste (page 310), apricots, cherries, sweetened curd cheese with egg yolks, vanilla, and raisins – feel free to experiment.

Whisk the yeast into the milk, along with 1 tablespoon of the sugar. Cover and leave in a warm place for about 15 minutes, or until it looks bubbly and alive.

Now add the rest of the sugar, followed by the butter, egg yolks, vanilla, and salt and mix everything together very well. Add the flour and mix to a soft dough, then turn out onto a lightly floured surface and give it a gentle knead. You should end up with a rich, decadent dough that's almost good enough to eat raw. Don't eat it yet, though: cover and leave to proof for about 1½–2 hours, or until doubled in size.

Line a baking sheet with baking parchment. Pinch off 2-oz pieces of dough and use a rolling pin to gently roll out into 4-inch circles. Put 2 tablespoons of the filling in the center of each one, then bring the dough up around the filling and pinch it closed with your fingers. Place the buns next to each other, seam side down, on the baking sheet (they will merge as they rise). Cover with a clean kitchen towel and leave to proof for 30 minutes.

Preheat the oven to 400°F. Brush the buns with the beaten egg and bake for 20–30 minutes, until golden brown. Serve warm, either on their own or with a simple broth.

Fried flatbreads with cheese

SERVES 8

½ cup + 2 Tbsp kefir or fermented baked milk (page 64)

1¾ cups (220g) all-purpose flour

4 oz halloumi cheese, coarsely grated

5 oz feta cheese, crumbled

1 Tbsp finely chopped dill – optional

Good-quality lard or vegetable oil, for frying

These are similar to the Turkish stuffed flatbreads called *gozleme*, except that *gozleme* are cooked on a dry griddle or frying pan and then brushed with butter, whereas these are fried in lard or oil. In southwest Ukraine, they are called *pitinki* (the Russian diminutive of *pita*), and in Bulgaria they go by the name of *krstachky*.

The dough is often made using water or whey – if you've made some *syr* curd cheese (page 338), the leftover whey would be perfect here – but I find that kefir or buttermilk works very well too. The *pitinkis* you see here have been fried in lard: if you can get hold of some good-quality lard, ideally from a local farm, do try it! Otherwise, use vegetable oil or bake in a 400°F oven for 10–15 minutes and then brush with brown butter. Serve with a fresh salad for lunch.

Pour the kefir or fermented baked milk into a large bowl and gradually add the flour, mixing to make a firm dough. Turn out onto a well-floured surface and knead until smooth. Cover and leave to rest for at least 15 minutes.

Meanwhile, for the filling, combine the halloumi with the feta. If you want, you can add some dill or other herbs at this stage (I like to use a mix of dill, cilantro, green onions, and sorrel).

Using a rolling pin, roll out the dough as thinly as possible. Cover half of it with the cheese filling, leaving a ¾-inch border at the edges. Flip the other half of the dough over the filling and join the edges, then cut with a serrated pastry cutter or a knife into 6 x 4-inch rectangles. Pinch the edges together firmly with your fingers, making sure no air is trapped inside.

Heat a ½-inch depth of lard or oil in a large frying pan over medium-low heat. Add the flatbreads in batches, perhaps two at a time, depending on the size of your pan. Cook for 2 minutes, then turn and cook for 1 minute on the other side, until they are light golden and crispy. Drain on paper towels and eat while hot.

Transcarpathian buns with mushrooms

SERVES 5
(MAKES 10 BUNS)

Considered the national dumplings of Belarus, *kalduny* have a curious name that is a homonym for "wizards" in Ukrainian. However, it is thought that the name actually comes from the giant Tatar dumplings called *kundumy*, which were fried in lots of fat from fat-tailed sheep, rather than being boiled.

This Transcarpathian version has a similar name, *kolduny*, but is very different from both the Tatar and Belarus dumplings. The buns are unusual in that they are generally fried before being braised in a white creamy sauce, but I prefer them sauceless, simply steamed and served with some mushroom and pickle broth (page 144). Another excellent way to cook these is to pop them, cut side up, on top of a simmering stew (like the barley, bean and mushroom casserole on page 224), cover, and cook for 10–15 minutes – the bottoms will absorb the juices from the stew and the tops will be fluffy. The filled buns freeze well, too, and can be steamed from frozen.

½ oz dried porcini or wild mushrooms – optional

2 Tbsp vegetable oil

8 oz cremini or white button mushrooms, finely diced

1 onion, finely diced

Small handful of finely chopped dill

⅓ cup thinly sliced green onions and/or wild garlic

Sea salt and black pepper

DOUGH

½ cup kefir

1 egg

1 tsp fine sea salt

1 tsp superfine sugar or honey

½ tsp baking soda

2 cups (250g) all-purpose flour

If using dried mushrooms, soak them in hot water for 30 minutes, then drain, leaving behind any sandy residue. Finely chop the reconstituted mushrooms.

Heat the oil in a frying pan over medium heat. Add the mushrooms and cook for about 5 minutes, stirring from time to time. Now add the diced onion, season lightly with salt, and turn down the heat to medium-low. Cook, stirring regularly, until the onion softens and starts to brown. Add the reconstituted dried mushrooms, if using, along with the dill and green onions and/or wild garlic. Season with salt and pepper – the filling should be well seasoned – then leave to cool.

Meanwhile, make the dough. In a large bowl, whisk the kefir, egg, salt, and sugar or honey together until smooth. Whisk in the baking soda and quickly add the flour, using a wooden spoon to mix, then use your hands to bring together into a dough. On a lightly floured surface, briefly knead the dough, until it is soft and pillowy. Leave to rest for about 5 minutes.

Flour the surface again and use a rolling pin to roll out the dough to a thin rectangle about 12 x 8 inches. Spoon the cooled filling over the bottom half of the dough, then roll it up quite firmly, tucking in the dough at each end. Cut the dough sausage crosswise into ¾-inch slices – you should end up with 10 buns. (At this stage, they freeze well, if you want to cook them some time later.)

Now lightly oil a steamer or colander and set it over a large pan of boiling water. Put in the buns, cut side up, cover with a lid, and steam for about 15 minutes.

Tatar pasta bows with garlic yogurt and walnuts

SERVES 2

---

2 eggs

1⅔ cup (200g) all-purpose flour or 1½ cups (200g) '00' pasta flour

1–2 garlic cloves, crushed or finely grated

½ cup + 2 Tbsp yogurt

4 oz (1 cup) very fresh walnuts (or pecans)

7 Tbsp butter, clarified butter, or ghee

Sea salt

Called *salma*, this is one of the simplest, yet most unusual pasta dishes. I first ate it with Amina Kadyr, a Tatar woman from Alexandrivka, a village close to the Sea of Azov. It was served with a choice of two toppings: butter and a garlicky homemade yogurt (*katyk*), or butter and crushed walnuts. I was greedy and piled on both! As the rest of this dish is so easy, it's well worth making the pasta yourself. Please use only the best, freshest nuts, and make sure you taste them before you toast them; if they are stale or rancid, this simple dish will be ruined.

I have also tried using beurre noisette, which works well with the yogurt: simply put about 5 tablespoons of butter in a light-colored saucepan and warm it gently, taking it off the heat as soon as it starts turning a deeper shade of golden brown and smelling nutty. Toss the pasta in the brown butter before drizzling with the garlic yogurt and scattering with the crushed walnuts.

In a large bowl, lightly beat the eggs with ¼ cup of water, then gradually add the flour. Mix with a wooden spoon at first, then use your hands to bring together into a dough. Turn out onto a well-floured surface and knead until you have a tight, smooth dough. Cover with a clean kitchen towel and let it rest for 15–30 minutes.

In a small bowl, stir the garlic into the yogurt and season really well with salt.

To toast the nuts, you can just toss them in a dry frying pan over a medium-low heat until golden brown, but they'll toast more evenly in the oven. To do this, scatter them over a baking sheet and toast in a preheated 350°F for about 10 minutes. Coarsely crush or roughly chop the nuts.

Divide the dough in half and flour the surface well. Using a pasta machine or rolling pin, roll out the dough as thinly as you can into a sheet about 12 x 8 inches. Cut into ten strips lengthwise and then cut crosswise on the diagonal to create 1¼ x ¾-inch diamond shapes. Pinch each pasta diamond in the middle to make a bow. (At this stage you can spread out the pasta bows on a tray and leave to dry overnight, then keep them in an airtight container for up to a month.)

Cook the pasta in a pan of well-salted boiling water for 2 minutes, or until it rises to the surface – it should be pleasantly al dente.

Meanwhile, melt the butter in a large frying pan over medium heat. Drain the pasta well in a colander, then toss briefly in the butter to coat. Serve with the garlic yogurt and the nuts and let people choose their own topping(s).

Spelt dumplings with kraut and caramelized onions

SERVES 2
(MAKES 16 DUMPLINGS)

---

2 onions

2 Tbsp canola oil

6 oz sauerkraut

2 cups (210g) spelt flour

1½ Tbsp butter (or more, to taste)

Sea salt

Yogurt or crème fraîche and pickles, to serve

A close cousin of *pierogi* dumplings, *varenyky* take their name from *varyty*, meaning "to boil," so they are literally "boiled ones." I never would have thought to use a spelt dough for this kind of dumpling, but I tried some near Lviv and got hooked – this is how dumplings might have been a long time ago, before industrialization made white flour ubiquitous.

The spelt flour gives the dumplings a deep flavor, and I never feel guilty eating them as they are so nutritious. They are not as melt-in-the mouth as regular *varenyky*, so be prepared for more chewiness. I like to eat these doused in butter and thick yogurt, with pickled jalapeños or some homemade chile paste (page 59) on the side.

Please read through the recipe before you get started, as you need to work quite fast with spelt dough.

First slice the onions, not too thinly. Heat the oil in a pan over low heat and add the onions and a pinch of salt – this will help to tease out the water from the onions, making them less likely to burn. Cook for about 10 minutes, covered with a lid or a cartouche (circle of baking parchment) to help things along. Keep an eye on them and stir from time to time, adding a splash of water and scraping the bottom of the pan if they start to look a bit dry.

When they're ready, the caramelized onions should be soft, dark, and fragrant. If they look a little watery, drain off the excess liquid – the dumpling filling has to be as dry as possible. (As caramelizing onions takes a little while, I often make a big batch that I can keep in the fridge and use for a myriad of dishes – in my son's sausage sandwiches, omelettes, and so on – over the next week.)

Drain the sauerkraut well, squeezing it out in a colander (put the juice back into the jar). Stir the kraut into the caramelized onions – you should have roughly 10 ounces of filling. I like half kraut and half onion, but feel free to vary these proportions, depending on how sour your kraut is: if it is very sour, use less of it. Once you've got your filling how you want it, set it aside.

Lightly flour a baking sheet and put a large pan of salted water on to boil.

Now for the dough. Once this dough is made, it loses its binding powers very quickly, so I recommend making half at a time. Put ¼ cup of water into a bowl and mix in half of the flour to make a rough dough. Turn out onto a floured surface and knead briefly to combine.

Roll the dough into a sausage shape and divide evenly into 8 pieces with a knife or dough scraper. Flatten each piece with the palm of your hand, then use a rolling pin to roll out into a circle as thin as you can manage. Now put a tablespoon of the filling in the center of each circle and fold in half to make a half-moon, crimping the edges together well. Put the dumplings on the baking sheet as you go along and cover with a damp kitchen towel so they don't dry out.

Make the other half of the dough in the same way, then shape and fill the rest of the dumplings, so you end up with 16.

One by one, gently drop the dumplings into the pan of boiling water, using a slotted spoon to make sure none of them get stuck to the bottom. Boil for about 6–8 minutes – they will float to the top when they're ready.

Put the butter in a serving bowl and have it by the stove, ready for the cooked dumplings. (My grandmother called the resulting melted butter *krynychka*, "a well," just to give you an idea of how much she actually used!) Lift out the dumplings with the slotted spoon, then pop them into the bowl and toss gently in the butter. Serve with yogurt or crème fraîche and some pickles.

Dumplings with beans and potato

SERVES 4–6
(MAKES 30 DUMPLINGS)

Soft, comforting *varenyky* dumplings are known and loved by everybody in Ukraine. I love this rather unusual butter bean version; although very similar in flavor to classic potato-filled *varenyky*, somehow these feel like less hassle to make. If you don't have any cooked potato for the filling, add some fried diced mushrooms instead. Conversely, it will also work with just leftover potato – if the potato's first life was as buttery, creamy mash, you might not even need the egg yolk. This same dough works for sweet *varenyky* too – try seasonal berries or slivers of apricot as a filling. The amount of dough to filling is always roughly 1:1.

DOUGH

1 small egg

1½ cups (175g) all-purpose flour or 1⅓ cups (175g) '00' pasta flour

FILLING

8 oz (1⅓ cups) drained butter beans (from 1 x 15-oz can)

½ cup cooked potato (baked or leftover mash)

1 egg yolk

Handful of chopped dill

Sea salt

Fine semolina or flour, for dusting

2 Tbsp vegetable oil

2 oz *salo* (page 338), *lardo*, or pancetta, diced

1 small onion, diced

1 Tbsp butter

Crème fraîche or sour cream, to serve

To make the dough, whisk the egg with ⅓ cup of water in a bowl, then gradually mix in the flour to make a rough dough. Turn out onto a well-floured surface, leaving any dry flakes of dough behind in the bowl. Knead until the dough stops sticking to your hands and is firm and elastic. Wrap in plastic wrap and leave to rest for at least 15 minutes – this will relax the gluten and make it easier to roll it out.

Meanwhile, for the filling, blitz the beans to a paste in a blender or food processor. Transfer to a bowl and add the potato, egg yolk, and a good pinch of salt. Work the mixture with a potato masher to bring everything together, then stir in the dill.

Now roll the dough into a sausage shape, then cut evenly into 30 little pillows of dough (each about 1¼ x ¾ inch).

Dust a tray or large plate with semolina or flour. On a flour-dusted surface, use a rolling pin to roll out each pillow of dough into a 3¼-inch circle. Place a teaspoonful of filling in the center, then pinch the edges of the circle together to close the dumpling, taking care not to trap any air inside. Put the dumplings on the tray or plate and keep covered with a damp kitchen towel to prevent their drying out.

Heat the oil in a frying pan over medium-low heat and add the *salo*, *lardo,* or pancetta. As soon as it starts to release its fat, add the onion and cook, stirring often, until everything looks deliciously crisp and golden.

Put the butter into a large bowl and have it by the stove, ready for the cooked dumplings. Now, working in two batches, gently slip the dumplings into a large pan of salted boiling water, giving them a gentle stir so they don't stick to the pan. Cook them for about 5 minutes – they will float to the top when they're ready. Lift out with a slotted spoon, then pop into the bowl and toss so they are slicked with butter. Scatter the crisp onion and *salo* mixture on top and serve with crème fraîche or sour cream.

Lazy dumplings with green beans, poppy seeds, and crispy shallots

SERVES 2 NEWLY CONVERTED *SYR*-HATERS (MAKES 12 DUMPLINGS)

By *syr*, Ukrainians mean a particular curd cheese, standing somewhere between cottage and ricotta cheese, made from raw milk at home and used for everything from spreading on rye bread to filling dumplings. So important is *syr* that it has also come to be a generic word for all cheeses.

Traditionally, Ukrainian mothers knew that *syr* was good for their children's bones and teeth, but my friend Katrya detested it. Her mum kept trying to sneak *syr* into sweet treats that Katrya might be persuaded to eat, but all her attempts failed miserably. Then one day she made *syr* into savory little curd cheese cushions… and, lo and behold, Katrya has been happily eating these Ukrainian cousins of Italian *malfatti* with butter and herbs ever since.

You don't have to abandon this fabulous dish in the colder seasons, either – just substitute the beans with winter greens. Some feta or other salty cheese can be added too, if you like.

DUMPLINGS

4 oz *syr* curd cheese (page 338) or well-drained ricotta

⅔ cup (75g) all-purpose flour

1 egg

Large handful of finely chopped dill

8 oz green beans, tops trimmed

⅓ cup sunflower or vegetable oil

2 shallots, thinly sliced

1 Tbsp all-purpose flour

2 Tbsp clarified butter (or butter with a splash of oil)

Pinch of poppy seeds

Sea salt and black pepper

For the dumplings, gently mix together the curd cheese or ricotta, flour, egg, and dill, then season with salt and pepper – it will be quite a wet dough. Turn out onto a lightly floured surface and carefully knead until it is no longer sticky, then cover with a clean kitchen towel and leave to rest while you get on with the beans and onions.

Cook the green beans to your liking: for crisp-tender, drop into boiling water and cook for 2 minutes; I prefer my beans softer, so I boil them for at least 4 minutes. Drain and set aside.

To make the crispy shallots, pour the oil into a frying pan over low heat. Just before you are ready to fry, toss the shallots in flour seasoned with salt, then shake off any excess and drop them into the hot oil. Cook until they are golden brown, but be careful not to take them too far, or they will taste acrid. Drain on paper towels.

Now, on a lightly floured surface, gently shape the dumpling dough into a 10-inch sausage and cut it into 12 pieces. With floured hands, lightly coax each piece into a dumpling about 2½ x ¾ inch. Bring a large saucepan of salted water to a boil, then slip in the dumplings, in batches, and cook for 2–3 minutes – they will float to the surface when they're done. Drain well in a colander.

Melt the clarified butter (or butter and oil) in a large frying pan over medium heat. Add the dumplings and gently toss for a few minutes, until they are a light golden color, then add the green beans to the pan and stir to warm through.

Serve the dumplings and green beans with the crispy shallots, poppy seeds, and some black pepper.

On *varenyky*

Whenever I find myself idly contemplating what my death-row dish might be, I end up deciding on my mother's *varenyky* dumplings – stuffed dumplings that take their name from *varyty* ("to boil"). She makes a dough from white flour, egg, and water and then rolls it out very thinly by hand. For the filling, she seasons homemade curd cheese heavily with salt and whisks in an egg yolk or two. The dough is then cut into squares before being filled and sealed to make delicate triangular dumplings. Boiled briefly in salted water and dropped into a *krynychka* ("well") of melted butter in a bowl, they are served with cool sour cream. One by one, they slip into your mouth, seamlessly, eagerly. I know I am full after twenty, but I cannot stop – I once ate fifty at one sitting!

Ukrainians' love for *varenyky* is old and deep-rooted. In a famous scene from Nikolai Gogol's story *The Night Before Christmas*, set in 1831, the protagonist, Vakula, is determined to find and confront the devil, who has stolen the crescent moon. When he goes to see an old witch doctor called Paunchy Patsiuk, the dastardly Patsiuk (whose name means "rat" in Ukrainian) is sitting on the floor in full Cossack attire, legs crossed, slurping noodles. His next course is *varenyky*, but his approach to eating these is quite different: "Patsiuk opened his mouth wide, looked at the dumplings, and opened his mouth still wider. Just then a dumpling flipped out of the bowl, plopped into the sour cream, turned over on the other side, jumped up and went straight into Patsiuk's mouth."

So significant are *varenyky* in Ukrainian culture that I could have written a whole chapter on the many ways they are cooked, served, and eaten. First, though, I want to talk about a variant that may in fact be much closer to the dumplings Patsiuk dispatched into his mouth using his magic powers.

>>

A few years ago, I visited Bohdan Komarnytsky and his family at their small, rustic home near Lviv – it was almost like a museum of Ukrainian peasant life. There was a small spelt field in the back garden and, right before my eyes, Bohdan milled the spelt grain he'd grown himself into fresh flour and we talked of long-forgotten grains and flours.

Prior to the twentieth century, white flour would have mainly been reserved for the nobility, as peasants couldn't afford to sieve out the bran (which would have made up a significant proportion of the flour) – although it turns out, of course, that the less refined flour was richer in nutrients and supplied the energy needed for working in the fields. Then, when the Soviets introduced collectivized farming and the food supply was more industrialized, bleached white flour became the norm. Buckwheat flour, which featured heavily in early Ukrainian recipe books, also went out of favor.

Bohdan promised us that after we ate dumplings made from his spelt flour, we would not feel heavy and tired, but rather full of energy and ready for a long day with a scythe in a field...or for tackling the devil! Initially I was quite skeptical. Even though I knew that spelt was more easily digested than wheat, and appreciated the health advantages of freshly ground whole-grain flours, I just didn't think the dumplings would be quite as delicious as their white-flour counterparts.

His wife briskly made the dough – you have to be quick when you're working with spelt flour, as its binding properties seem to dissipate by the minute – and filled the dumplings with chopped sauerkraut. Feeling tired after a six-hour drive from Transcarpathia, I ate a plate of dumplings and prepared myself for a post-dumpling nap. But Bohdan was right! I felt surprisingly energized for the rest of the evening.

While the flour used for *varenyky* may have changed, the fillings have remained pretty constant. Vegetarian fillings seem to dominate. One of the most common is mashed-potato dumplings that closely resemble Polish *pierogi*;

they are traditionally served with plenty of *shkvarky* (fried *salo* lardons) and lashings of sour cream. In western Ukraine, curd cheese is mixed into the potato, and in central Ukraine baked potato is mashed together with boiled beans. Sweetened curd-cheese dumplings are also ubiquitous, though it's the savory versions I pine for.

One of the most exquisite fillings for *varenyky* involves fine strands of sauerkraut, gently cooked with onion and porcini mushrooms; fresh cabbage and mushrooms is another popular choice, especially in the north. As for meat, some old recipes mention pork meat and lung as a filling, but I personally have never come across it; I have eaten *varenyky* filled with pork liver, however. In Besarabia, by the Danube River, fish is used – sturgeon historically, and carp nowadays.

Varenyky can also be served as a dessert, usually filled with fresh fruit or berries and sprinkled with a little sugar. In the northwest of Ukraine, June sees the dense green forests flush with sweet bilberries, also known as huckleberries. These are eagerly folded into rounds of dough, boiled, and then served with butter and sugar. The same fate awaits pitted sour cherries, strawberries, and slices of apricot all over Ukraine.

In Poltava, baking soda is added to the dough and the dumplings are steamed rather than boiled. Nearer Moldova, later in the year, you might find *varenyky* stuffed with pumpkin, apple, and nuts, served with melted butter and jam. There are records of a honeyed poppyseed filling too – but then this paste is so luxuriously tasty, it is no surprise it gets used in so many sweet recipes.

And in the early twentieth century, an unusual dumpling used to be made by Hutsul women in the Carpathian mountains: *varenyky* filled with sour cherries and a little sugar would be covered in fried *salo* (fatty cured pork) and its fat. It seemed such an odd, wild combination to me, but then I remembered Elisabeth Luard's words, in *European Peasant Cookery*: "The divorce of salt and sweet came late to Europe. For centuries meat puddings

>>

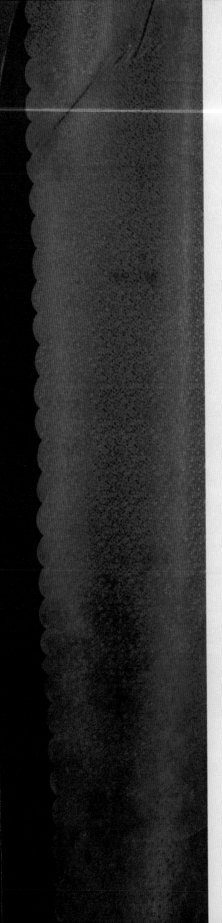

and dumplings were as likely to be flavored with plums and raisins, nuts, and honey, as they were with herbs and salt."

Despite all the changes and rediscoveries, dumplings like *varenyky* are still so popular and cherished because of their irresistible combination of a humble yet silky dough, a simple filling – whether a lovely, lactic curd cheese, tasty mashed potato, or sweet and tart berries – and the skill and labor that go into shaping them. The latter is nothing less than a manifestation of love by those who make them, usually our mothers – an attribute common to hundreds of other dumplings all over the world.

Vegetables

FROM FIELD AND FOREST

When I was a teenager living in Cyprus, and later in the UK, I always felt really hurt and offended when people in my new home countries suggested that Ukrainian food must be all about potatoes and overcooked cabbage.

———————————————————

Mind you, the potatoes my aunt grows are the best I have ever tasted: they need nothing more than to be simply boiled and enjoyed with a slick of oil or butter and a little salt, the quality is just so good. And the young cabbages are so delicious. My mother and grandmother would never overcook cabbage when it shouldn't be done that way, such as in borsch – but sometimes cabbage, slowly braised until it is meltingly soft, is one of the most delicious, nutritious, and comforting things. So now I have proudly embraced both potatoes and cabbage.

Ukraine is bigger than France, and it is as regional. Where I'm from, in the south, we have a really hot climate and enormous flavor-bomb tomatoes, all kinds of eggplant, zucchini, peppers, and a huge variety of herbs flourish in the warm sunshine. Go a little further north, and you get wild mushrooms and berries. People in Ukraine used to eat a lot of vegetable-based dishes. Right up until the 1950s, meat was treated as a luxury, and those who kept animals killed and ate them seasonally, using traditional preservation methods to make the meat last the whole year.

When I used to work in a restaurant, I found prepping endless boxes of vegetables very mindful and therapeutic. Cooking vegetables is still one of the most satisfying things I do in my kitchen at home, and I find it even more satisfying now that I am married to a man who has been vegetarian since he was ten years old. Because of him, I am constantly on the lookout for vegetarian Eastern European dishes (still trying to impress!). You will find a lot of my favorites here, like potato cakes stuffed with bean paste, cauliflower fritters, and a raw turnip salad. Most of them are simple to prepare too – dishes that allow vegetables to taste of their wonderful selves.

Cauliflower fritters

SERVES 4

---

1 small cauliflower

Vegetable oil, for frying

1 egg, beaten

½ cup whole milk

½ cup (60g) buckwheat or all-purpose flour

Sea salt and black pepper

DILL AND GARLIC MAYONNAISE

⅔ cup mayonnaise

1 garlic clove, finely grated

Handful of finely chopped dill

A simple batter is used all over Ukraine for frying all sorts of things, from chicken or pork schnitzel to whole river fish. I love vegetables fried in this way, and cauliflower is especially good. Normally, plain white flour is used, but buckwheat flour was a popular choice in the past and I tend to use it instead of wheat flour – it is healthier, and much more flavorsome. You can use the batter in this recipe for vegetables other than cauliflower. Normally the fritters are eaten just as they are, but I like them with a spoonful of dill-and-garlic-spiked mayo. If you come across some good-quality chipotle mayo, that wouldn't go amiss either.

Cut the cauliflower into small florets, keeping any sprightly smaller leaves too. Blanch the cauliflower and its leaves in a pan of boiling, salted water. Take the leaves out after about 2 minutes, and the florets after 5 minutes. Refresh both in cold water, then drain well and pat dry with paper towels.

Heat ¼ cup of oil in a large frying pan over medium heat: it should cover the base of the pan; if not add a little more.

If you are using buckwheat flour, make the batter just before you are ready to fry as it becomes gloopier by the minute. In a bowl, whisk the egg with the milk, then add the flour and whisk until smooth. Season well with salt and pepper.

Drop four pieces of cauliflower into the batter bowl at a time, making sure they are all thickly coated.

When the oil is really hot, bring the bowl over to the pan (otherwise everything will get super-messy!) and pop the batter-coated pieces of cauliflower into the pan. Depending on the size of your pan, you should be able to fry between 4 and 8 fritters at a time. When they are golden all over, drain on paper towels. You might need to wipe out the pan with paper towels and add more oil in between batches.

For the dill and garlic mayonnaise, simply combine all the ingredients in a small bowl.

Serve the cauliflower fritters with the garlic-spiked dill mayo.

Carpathian beets and mushrooms

SERVES 4 AS A SIDE

¾ oz dried wild mushrooms

3 beets

2 Tbsp canola oil

6 shallots, halved and then thinly sliced lengthwise

3 Tbsp blackcurrant vinegar or red wine vinegar

2 garlic cloves, finely grated

Sea salt and black pepper

Marjoram or oregano leaves, to serve

This is my version of *shukhy*, a Christmas dish cooked by Hutsul highlanders and other people in western Ukraine. Blackcurrant vinegar goes wonderfully with the earthy beets, but you could substitute any flavorsome vinegar. Add some herbs at the end, if you like – tarragon would not be out of place, I feel, even if it does stray from the traditional offering. This is usually served cold, as part of a festive feast.

Soak the mushrooms in some hot water for at least 30 minutes, then drain well, leaving behind any sandy residue.

Put the whole unpeeled beets into a saucepan of salted cold water, then bring to a boil and cook for 40 minutes–1 hour, until they can be easily pierced with a knife. (You could roast the beets instead, if you like, but I think there is something pure and fresh about a boiled beet.) Drain and, when they are cool enough to handle, rub off the skins and cut into thinnish slices and then into strips.

Heat the oil in a frying pan over medium-low heat. Throw in the shallots and cook until they start taking on a little color, then add the mushrooms and cook for a minute or so. Finally, add the vinegar and the garlic and switch off the heat. Season to taste with salt and pepper.

Mix the onion and mushroom mixture with the beets, then allow to cool. Garnish with marjoram or oregano leaves before serving.

Cucumber, yogurt, and nutmeg

SERVES 2 AS A SIDE

⅓ cup yogurt

A generous grating of nutmeg

9 oz English cucumbers (about 2 medium ones), thinly sliced

Sea salt and black pepper

This recipe comes from the Ukrainian and Polish *cucina povera* tradition – it used to be made by peasants, and so rich landowners haughtily called it *mizeria* ("misery").

What sets this version apart is the more modern grating of nutmeg, an unexpected and delicious addition. This makes a wonderfully refreshing accompaniment to roast or grilled meats, or serve it with a selection of other vegetable dishes.

Put the yogurt into a large bowl and season it very well with salt, remembering that the watery cucumber will dilute the seasoning. Grate in the nutmeg and add some black pepper too, if you like.

Add the cucumber and mix well. This may be served straight away, but it can also be made a few hours in advance.

Little peppers with tomato sauce

SERVES 6 AS A SIDE

This dish – *manja* – can be eaten as soon as it's cooked, but the sauce can also be preserved for winter. There are numerous variations and countless claims about its origins: *mangia* means "eat" in Italian, and Bulgarians and the Gagauz both make it, as do Romanians, Moldovans, and people from southwest Ukraine.

In Vylkove, right on the border with Romania, Vera Kagayeva gave me a version of this recipe containing eggplant, which sounded delicious, but I also loved her idea of serving the sauce with fried green peppers. I like to use Padrón or similar peppers, but if you can't get them, just use the smallest green peppers you can find. You don't have to dice everything finely, as I do here – the original recipe calls for roughly chopped veggies, and this is quite a rustic dish.

If you would like to preserve the sauce for winter, add slightly more salt and vinegar, then transfer it to sterilized jars and cover the surface with a protective layer of oil before sealing.

---

4 Tbsp vegetable oil

1 whole garlic bulb, cloves separated and peeled

1 onion, finely diced

1 red bell pepper, finely diced

1 small carrot, finely diced

3 large, ripe tomatoes, finely chopped or grated

½ Tbsp sherry vinegar or red wine vinegar

25–30 Padrón, shishito, or frigitelli (peperoncini) peppers *or* 6 small green peppers

1 Tbsp unrefined sunflower oil (or walnut or pumpkin seed oil)

Sea salt

Bread and feta or other salty cheese, to serve – optional

Heat half the vegetable oil in a large frying pan over medium-low heat and add the garlic cloves. Do not panic about the amount of garlic – it will mellow, becoming quite sweet. Cook until the garlic softens, then add the onion and cook, stirring from time to time, until it softens and turns light golden. I sometimes put a lid or cartouche (cut out a circle of baking parchment about the same size as your pan, then wet it) over the onion to speed things up.

Now add the red bell pepper and carrot and cook for 5 minutes or so, until the carrot starts to soften. Add the tomatoes, season well with salt, and cook for another 10–15 minutes, until the tomatoes break down into the sauce. If the pan starts looking a bit dry, add a splash of water. Finally, add the vinegar and cook for 5 minutes. Taste the sauce – it should be well seasoned and slightly sharp.

Wash and drain the green peppers, without drying them too thoroughly – you want a little water to cling to them so they will steam-fry. Heat the remaining vegetable oil in a large frying pan (that you have a lid for) over high heat and carefully toss the peppers into the pan – they might be a bit explosive! Cook for a minute or so, shaking the pan every so often, then cover with the lid and cook for a few more minutes. When they're done, the peppers should have wilted and be charred and blistered in places.

Lay the peppers on a large plate and pour the warm or cold sauce over, trying to avoid the stems of the peppers, then drizzle with the sunflower oil. To eat, scoop up the sauce with the peppers or spread it on bread, crushing the soft garlic into it with a knife, then place the peppers on top.

Beet leaf rolls with buckwheat and mushrooms

SERVES 4
(MAKES 16 ROLLS)

½ cup toasted buckwheat

2 Tbsp vegetable oil

8 oz mushrooms, finely diced

2 onions, 1 diced and 1 sliced

1 carrot, scrubbed and coarsely grated

Leaves from 16 medium beets (or 16 chard leaves), stalks removed and reserved

1 lb ripe tomatoes
or
1 x 14.5-oz can of diced tomatoes

2 Tbsp crème fraîche

Sea salt and black pepper

Crusty bread, to serve

In the Carpathian highlands, in summertime, Hutsul women often use beet leaves to make a variation of *holubtsi* ("little doves"), the iconic Ukrainian dish of cabbage rolls. The beet leaves are left in the sun to wilt slightly, to make rolling them a little easier, but I find that when you buy beets with leaves on, the leaves are often pretty limp already, so all they need is a quick wash. You could also include some chopped cooked chestnuts to the filling, if you like – they add a wonderful texture and flavor.

If you can find only raw, green buckwheat, toast it first, as described on page 337, then leave it to cool before cooking.

Cook the buckwheat in a saucepan of salted boiling water for about 10 minutes, or until cooked through but not falling apart. Drain well and set aside in a bowl.

Heat 1 tablespoon of the oil in a frying pan over medium heat, add the mushrooms and cook until they brown a little. Scoop them out into the bowl of buckwheat. Turn the heat down to medium-low and add the diced onion to the pan, along with a pinch of salt. Cook until it softens and starts to turn golden, then add the carrot and cook for about 2 minutes, letting it color a little. Tip the contents of the frying pan into the bowl, mix well, and season with salt and pepper, then leave the filling to cool slightly.

Lay a beet leaf on your worktop and put 1 heaping teaspoon of the filling close to the stalk end, then flip the bottom of the leaf up and over the filling. Fold in the sides and roll up as tightly as possible, leaving the finished roll on the worktop, seam side down. Repeat with the rest of the beet leaves and filling.

Choose a saucepan or cast-iron casserole with a lid that will hold the beet leaf rolls snugly in a single layer. Add the rest of the oil and place over medium heat, then add the sliced onion and cook until soft and mellow. Finely chop the beet stalks, add to the pan, and cook, stirring, for another minute or so. If you are using fresh tomatoes, cut them in half and grate them on the coarse side of a box grater, discarding the skins. Add the tomatoes to the pan and cook for about 5 minutes, or until they have broken down into a sauce, then whisk in the crème fraîche and season with salt and pepper. Turn the heat down to low and carefully add the rolls, seam side down, then cover and cook for 15 minutes.

Serve with plenty of crusty bread to mop up the juices.

Raw turnip and green onion salad with yogurt dressing

SERVES 2

---

12 oz turnips (4–5 small ones)

Juice of ½ lemon

½ cup yogurt (or crème fraîche)

2 green onions, very
thinly sliced

Sea salt and black pepper,
to taste

Turnip – that seemingly humble, underrated vegetable! So British, extremely Slovakian, and also very Ukrainian. This dish is another one from Zinovia Klynovetska's 1913 cookbook, *Dishes and Drinks of Ukraine*.

This salad is akin to a light, vibrant rémoulade of sorts, and the raw turnip is a particular delight. It is good as a side salad, but I also love piling it on a chunk of sourdough bread or toast when I want a healthy snack.

Peel the turnips, then cut them into thin matchsticks or grate on the coarse side of a box grater. Place in a bowl.

Here is a little tip for making salad dressings if you like to use flaky sea salt: squeeze the lemon juice into a bowl, then add the salt and whisk – the lemon's acidity will help to dissolve the salt. Now whisk in the yogurt and some pepper, if you like.

Pour the dressing over the turnips and toss to coat thoroughly, then stir through the green onions and serve.

Tomato and mulberry salad

SERVES 4 AS A SIDE

4 oz mulberries or blackberries

3 Tbsp cider vinegar
or blackcurrant vinegar

2 Tbsp unrefined sunflower oil
(or walnut or pumpkin seed oil)

1 small mild red onion,
thinly sliced

1 lb large ripe tomatoes, such
as beefsteak, cut into wedges

Handful of purple (or green)
basil leaves

Sea salt and black pepper,
to taste

Like me, food writer Marianna Dushar is partial to tomato and fruit combinations. When I visited her in Lviv, she made a tomato salad with the sweetest purple mulberries.

Only with hindsight do I understand how lucky I was as a child. In August, the berries would be everywhere: a black carpet of them, right outside our house. We thought they were more of a nuisance, not least because our feet would be black by the end of the day, which meant a telling-off when we got home. Now I would consider myself lucky to find a basket of mulberries and pay through the roof for them. If you struggle to find them too, just use blackberries instead.

Take a tablespoonful of the berries and squash them with a spoon in a bowl, then add the vinegar, oil, and salt and pepper and whisk it all together. Taste for seasoning: the dressing should be sour, sweet, and salty.

Add the onion to the dressing and leave it there for 10 minutes or so to mellow, if you have time.

Put the tomatoes on a plate, drizzle with the dressing, and scatter with the basil leaves and the rest of the berries.

Apple, celery, and kraut salad

SERVES 4 AS A SIDE

---

14 oz sauerkraut

½ lb sweet apples

2 celery ribs

1 small shallot

2 quick-fermented cucumbers (page 26) or pickles in brine

1 fermented apple (page 38) – optional

2–3 Tbsp unrefined sunflower or pumpkin seed oil

Small handful of celery leaves

This is my mum's version of a winter slaw and it is addictive and "moreish," especially if you have made your own kraut (page 28). It is also good for you.

I think substituting the apples with ripe pears or even Asian pears (nashi) and fennel for the celery would also work beautifully.

Drain the sauerkraut well and put it into a large bowl.

Core and thinly slice the apples, then thinly slice the celery, shallot, cucumbers or pickles, and fermented apple, if using.

Add these to the bowl, drizzle with the oil, and gently toss everything together.

Transfer to a serving dish and scatter with the celery leaves.

Zucchini with herbaceous *lyok* dressing

SERVES 4

LYOK DRESSING

4 sprigs of thyme or lemon thyme, leaves picked

Handful of tarragon leaves

Handful of dill fronds and stalks

Handful of parsley leaves and stalks

1 garlic clove

6 Tbsp cider vinegar (or any other mild fruit vinegar)

2 tsp honey or superfine sugar

¼ cup vegetable oil

2 medium zucchini, sliced into rounds

Sea salt and black pepper, to taste

A friend cooked this for me, in her summer kitchen in Kakhovka, southern Ukraine. In the south, we are well known for our *lyok* (garlic and herb pastes). They are generally used in broths, but here a combination of soft tarragon, dill, and parsley with woody thyme, makes for a flavor unlike any I have ever experienced.

I urge you to try this dish – you will not regret it. Serve with some simple boiled potatoes or as a part of a summer lunch.

For the *lyok* dressing, you can either chop the herbs and garlic finely by hand or use a mortar and pestle to pound them to a paste, then add the vinegar, honey or sugar, and seasoning – all vinegars are different, so adjust how much honey, salt, and pepper you add accordingly. Alternatively, you could just blitz everything together in a food processor. What you should end up with is a heady, herbaceous dressing: sweet, sour, salty, and a little spiky from the black pepper.

Heat the oil in a large frying pan and fry the zucchini on both sides until tender and golden. (You could also grill or roast them.) Pour the dressing over while the zucchini are still warm.

This dish is excellent at room temperature or cold, a perfect one to do in advance. If your thyme has flowers, sprinkle them over to make it even prettier.

Butter bean, red onion, and celery salad

SERVES 2

---

1 red onion, peeled

3 celery ribs, sliced

2 sprigs of thyme, leaves only

3 Tbsp mild vinegar (I use Moscatel)

1 Tbsp honey

1 x 15-oz can of butter beans, drained

Sea salt and black pepper

Crusty bread, to serve

I first ate this delicious salad in a summer kitchen in southern Ukraine, and now it is something I often throw together for an easy, light, and satisfying lunch. It is a very adaptable dish that you can make with any crunchy vegetable you have around, such as carrots, cabbage, cucumber, lettuce – anything goes. If you have time, you can leave the dressed onion, celery, and thyme in the fridge overnight to pickle slightly, then toss through the beans next day.

Cut the onion in half, then slice it thinly, going with the grain rather then cutting across it. Put the sliced onion in a colander in the sink and pour some boiling water over it, then briefly refresh under cold running water and drain well. Tip the onion into a bowl, then add the celery and thyme.

In a small bowl, mix ½ teaspoon of salt into the vinegar until completely dissolved, then stir in the honey and some black pepper. Taste the dressing and adjust accordingly – it should be strongly seasoned.

Pour the dressing over the onion, celery, and thyme and toss to coat everything well, then add the beans and mix well. Eat with a lovely crusty piece of bread.

Cabbage and cucumber salad

SERVES 4 AS A SIDE

---

1 tsp superfine sugar or honey

2 Tbsp cider vinegar or white wine vinegar

½ small white or sweetheart cabbage, thinly sliced

½ English cucumber

A slick of unrefined sunflower oil (or pumpkin seed or walnut oil)

Sea salt and black pepper

This is one of the most popular salads in Ukraine. It is very simple, but is made special by the use of nutty, unrefined sunflower oil. If you have trouble finding this, you can always mix a little sesame oil with a milder sunflower oil to replicate the effect, or use good-quality pumpkin seed or walnut oil instead. It goes really well with grilled fish and some new potatoes, crushed and tossed with wild garlic, sorrel, dill, and butter.

In a large bowl, whisk a scant tablespoon of sea salt and the sugar or honey into the vinegar until completely dissolved. Add the cabbage and massage well with your hands. This will soften the cabbage and pickle it ever so slightly. If you have time, leave it for 15 minutes.

Cut the cucumber in half lengthwise and scoop out the seeds, then slice thinly into half moons. Add the cucumber to the cabbage, mix, and season with black pepper, if you like – it should be quite punchy in flavor.

Finally drizzle with some strong, nutty oil and mix again.

Beets with apple and nuts

SERVES 4

---

3 medium beets

2 Tbsp sherry vinegar or fruit vinegar (I like blackcurrant best for this)

1 Tbsp canola, olive, or unrefined sunflower oil

1 Granny Smith apple

Handful of walnuts or pecans, lightly toasted

Sea salt and black pepper

This is absolutely delicious. It ticks so many boxes, especially if, like me, you crave zing and freshness after the indulgent and often heavy food of winter festivities. In fact, the Christmas season is a good time to make this for another reason: walnuts, which can go rancid quickly, tend to be fresher then. Pecans make a good substitute, but feel free to use any nut you love, or to add other vegetables, such as cabbage. Simplicity usually does it for me, though, more than ever these days.

This is considered to be a salad in Ukraine, but I have also come around to eating it in a very British way, more like a relish – as part of a ploughman's lunch, say, with cheese and bread.

You can roast the beets if you like, but I really enjoy the fresh flavor of boiled beets. Wash them really well, but leave the skins on. Pop them into a saucepan of cold water and bring to a boil, then simmer until cooked through. This could take 1 hour or even longer. Start checking them with the tip of a knife after 40 minutes – when they're ready, they should be fairly soft, with only a little bit of resistance. Drain and rinse under cold water. When they're cool enough to handle, peel off the skins with your hands.

In a large bowl, whisk ½ teaspoon of salt into the vinegar until it has dissolved. Whisk in the oil, then check for seasoning: the dressing should be well-seasoned, so add some pepper and don't skimp on the salt.

Now grate the beets on the coarse side of a box grater and drain well if they release a lot of liquid. Then do the same with the apple, leaving the core behind. Scoop them both into the bowl with the dressing and mix well, then crumble the nuts over.

Zucchini fritters

SERVES 5 AS PART
OF A BIGGER MEAL
(MAKES 10 FRITTERS)

1 lb zucchini

1 small egg, beaten

Large handful of finely
chopped dill

6 Tbsp self-rising flour

2 Tbsp vegetable oil

Sea salt and black pepper

Crème fraîche or yogurt,
to serve

People in Ukraine tend to make their fritters with finely grated vegetables, and I find a lot of comfort in the soft, almost sloppy result. The fritters you see in the photo were fried on a *pich* stove in a summer kitchen right by the Belarus border, and we ate them at a table outside, next to an enormous vegetable patch. Actually, it was more of a field than a patch, stretching out in front of us, right up to the neighboring woods. While we ate, we were regaled with stories about Belarus pensioners who come to the village in buses to go food shopping at the markets. Apparently the pensions in Belarus are much higher than in Ukraine, but the produce is worse. If the zucchini and potatoes at the local markets are as good as the ones from that vegetable patch, I would happily pack myself onto a bus and across the border to do my weekly shop.

These fritters are supposed to be soft and comforting. Sometimes, however, to add texture, I serve them sprinkled with crispy shallots. Thinly slice a few shallots, then leave them to pickle for at least an hour in a little rice or cider vinegar. Dry well, dust in flour, and shallow-fry in hot vegetable oil until crisp.

Grate the zucchini on a box grater, using the fine side that doesn't trap the bits in it! If your zucchini seem watery and full of seeds, grate the skin and flesh all the way round, but stop as soon as you get to the core – the seedy bit. If the zucchini are young, you can just grate the whole thing. (Whatever you do, you're aiming for 9 ounces (about 2 cups) grated zucchini to 6 tablespoons flour, so remember to adjust the amount of flour accordingly if you end up with more or less than that.)

Wrap the grated zucchini flesh in a clean kitchen towel and squeeze out as much moisture as possible, then tip into a bowl. Add the egg and mix thoroughly, then stir in the dill and flour and season generously with salt and pepper.

Heat the oil in a large frying pan over medium heat. When the oil is hot, drop tablespoonfuls of the fritter mixture into the pan, flattening them slightly. Fry for 2 minutes on one side with the lid on, then gently flip them over and cook for another minute. Serve with crème fraîche or yogurt.

"Black swan effect" peppers stuffed with apple, carrot, and rice

SERVES 4

Quite unusually for a Ukrainian, my friend Katrya has been a vegetarian for more than twenty years: as soon as she left home, she stopped eating meat. Her mother, Zhenia, was so upset that it turned into quite a scandal, and she insisted on regular blood tests to monitor Katrya's iron levels – which, of course, remained disconcertingly adequate. Eventually, Zhenia started cooking dishes that an average Ukrainian just could not imagine without meat. Stuffed peppers – with apple, instead of ground meat. Salad Olivier (more commonly known as Russian salad) – with apple, instead of sausage! Katrya described this development in terms of the "black swan effect," where a rare event has a big impact.

Now, when Katrya goes to other people's houses, she is never even slightly tempted by Russian salads full of processed sausage and meaty stuffed peppers. She sticks with her more delicate versions – and I, for one, am glad she does. These stuffed peppers are light and summery, and so delicious that you won't miss the meat at all.

FILLING

⅓ cup brown or white rice

2 Tbsp butter with a splash of oil

1 onion, finely diced

1 large carrot, finely diced

2 celery ribs, finely diced

4 oz (⅔ cup) corn kernels or peas

1 green apple, cored and diced

Small handful of thyme leaves

SAUCE

2 Tbsp butter with a splash of oil

1 onion, thinly sliced

3 garlic cloves, thinly sliced

2 large ripe tomatoes (or 1 x 14.5-oz can of diced tomatoes)

½ cup crème fraîche or thick heavy cream

¾ cup vegetable stock

A little sugar – optional

4 large red bell peppers

Sea salt and white pepper

Chopped parsley and dill, to serve

For the filling, boil the rice for 30 minutes if using brown rice, or 7 minutes if using white rice. Drain well and leave to cool. Heat the butter and oil in a large frying pan over medium-low heat. Add the onion, carrot, and celery and cook until soft and slightly golden, then stir in the rice, corn or peas, apple, and thyme. Season generously with salt and pepper – the filling should be very well seasoned, almost on the verge of being slightly over, as it will also serve as seasoning for the peppers.

For the sauce, heat the butter and oil in a frying pan over medium heat. Add the onion and cook for 5 minutes, until it softens and starts to turn golden. Add the garlic, turn down the heat to low, and cook gently for about 3–5 minutes to mellow its flavor. Grate in the tomatoes, discarding the skins (or add the canned tomatoes), and cook for 15 minutes, stirring from time to time. Whisk the crème fraîche or cream with the stock, then pour into the pan and stir in well. Season with salt, pepper, and perhaps a little sugar, if it needs it – the sauce should be silky and luscious.

Preheat the oven to 425°F. Cut the butts off the peppers and seed them, then stuff with the filling. Pour half the sauce into a baking dish that will snugly hold the peppers. Sit them upright in the dish, then pour the rest of the sauce over the top. Cover the dish tightly with a lid or foil and cook in the oven for 30 minutes. Take off the lid or foil and return to the oven for another 10 minutes, or until cooked through and golden. Serve with parsley and some dill... always with the dill...

ПЕРЕЦЬ ФАРШИРОВАНИЙ ЯБЛУКАМИ

Barley, bean, and mushroom casserole

SERVES 6-8

9 oz (1¼ cups) dried cannellini beans
or
2 x 15-oz cans of cannellini beans, drained

1½ oz dried wild or porcini mushrooms

3⅓ cups hot water

1 cup pearl barley

3 Tbsp vegetable oil

3½ Tbsp butter – optional

2 onions, diced

2 garlic cloves, finely chopped

2 Tbsp tomato paste

1 tsp sweet paprika

2¾ oz chanterelle mushrooms

Sea salt and black pepper

Chopped parsley, to serve

Although this casserole – *chovlent* in Ukrainian – hails from the Transcarpathian region of western Ukraine, the dish has Jewish origins. It can be made with meat, instead of the dried mushrooms and their soaking liquid (just poach some lamb or pork until tender and use the meat stock), but in this instance it makes for a brilliant, hearty vegetarian meal, one that is very popular during Lent, when some people abstain from eating meat. If there are any leftovers for another day, I like to mix it up a little and crumble some feta over the top.

If using dried beans, soak them overnight.

Next day, drain the beans and put them into a pot with plenty of cold unsalted water. Bring to a boil, then lower the heat and simmer gently (if the water is boiling too hard, the skins will start coming off) for about 50 minutes, or until soft, but not falling apart.

Soak the dried mushrooms in the hot water for about 30 minutes, then drain, reserving the soaking liquid but leaving behind any sandy residue. Squeeze as much water as you can out of the mushrooms and set them aside.

Put the pearl barley into a saucepan of cold salted water and bring to a boil, then turn down to a simmer and cook for about 20–30 minutes, or until just cooked. Drain and set aside (you can save the cooking liquid – barley water – and drink it chilled with some citrus juice, if you like).

Heat 2 tablespoons of the oil and half the butter (if using) in a flameproof casserole over low heat. Add the onions and a pinch of salt and cook slowly for about 10 minutes, until they start to turn golden. I find that a cartouche helps here – just cut out a baking parchment circle about the same size as the casserole, wet it, and put it over the onions – as it speeds up the process and saves you from burning them if you get distracted.

Now add the garlic, tomato paste, and paprika and cook for about 3 minutes, then pour in the reserved mushroom soaking liquid, turn up the heat to medium, and cook for another 3 minutes. Finally, add the pearl barley, beans, and reconstituted mushrooms, season to taste with salt and pepper, and cook for 10 minutes.

Meanwhile, fry the chanterelles in the remaining oil (and butter, if using) over medium-high heat, in batches, without turning them too often – you need to allow them to get nice and golden.

Serve the casserole with the fried mushrooms on top and a little parsley scattered over.

Vegetable casserole

SERVES 4

½ small celery root

1 large onion

1 carrot

About ¼ cup olive oil or good-quality sunflower oil

14 oz eggplant (1 large or 6 baby eggplants)

2 red bell peppers, cut into 1¼-inch chunks

7 oz green beans or yellow wax beans

10 oz ripe tomatoes, roughly chopped (or halved if small)

¼ Savoy or sweetheart cabbage

4 garlic cloves, crushed

Sea salt and black pepper

Chunks of good bread, to serve

Widespread in Bulgaria, Romania, and Moldova, this dish has made its way to Ukraine's southwestern border too.

It makes a perfect early autumn dish, when tomatoes and green beans are still around, and sweetheart cabbage and celery root are also in season to add weightiness.

Peel the celery root, discarding any bits of peel that have soil deeply ingrained in them, but keeping the clean peelings. Peel the onion and carrot, again keeping the peelings. Set the celery root, onion, and carrot aside for later. Put all the peelings into a stockpot or large saucepan with 1 quart of water and bring to a boil, then turn the heat down to low and simmer the stock for about 30 minutes. Take off the heat and leave to one side.

Cut the celery root, onion, and carrot into ½-inch dice. Heat a slug of the oil in a heavy-based pot over medium-low heat. Add the onion and carrot and brown them lightly, then transfer to a large bowl. Add the celery root to the pan and cook until golden at the edges, then add it to the bowl as well.

If using baby eggplants, steam-fry them whole: add some more oil to the pot and turn up the heat to medium-high. When the oil is really hot, throw in your eggplants and as soon as you hear them sizzle, cover with the lid. Let them cook, shaking the pot from time to time, for about 5 minutes, until they soften. If you are using a large eggplant, cut it into ¾-inch chunks and just fry in a little oil until golden. When the eggplant is done, transfer it to the bowl as well.

Add a little more oil to the pot if needed and fry the peppers over high heat until blistered and softened. Put into the bowl with the rest of the vegetables.

Next strain your vegetable stock into the pot and add the green or yellow beans. Bring to a boil, cover with the lid, and cook for 4 minutes – I like my beans soft, especially in a dish like this.

Now tip all the vegetables from the bowl back into the pot, add the tomatoes and season with salt and pepper to taste. Separate the cabbage leaves, cutting away any tough bits, and tear or cut them lengthwise. Pop the leaves on top and cover with the lid. Cook over medium heat for about 10 minutes, or until the cabbage leaves are tender.

Stir the cabbage leaves through the casserole, along with the raw garlic, then check for seasoning and serve with chunks of bread.

Braised cabbage of Sean's dreams

SERVES 6

---

1 small green cabbage

2 Tbsp canola oil

2 onions, thickly sliced

1½ tsp caraway seeds

1 large red bell pepper, thickly sliced

½ cup tomato juice (or use the juices from canned tomatoes)

¾ cup crème fraîche

1 Tbsp chopped parsley

Sea salt and black pepper

For a long time I had a real, deep-rooted complex about Ukraine's cabbage and potato dishes, all too often the only things people in the West associated with Eastern European cooking. But now I embrace them all – none more so than a delicious braised cabbage. This is my mother's recipe, and it is a pretty common one. When my Cornish friend Sean cooked it, the next day he texted me these beautiful words: "I cannot convey how much I loved the cabbage last night, so amazing. It goes so far to disprove the stereotype. I had dreams about it." Needless to say, that made my heart sing!

Serve this as an accompaniment to poultry or sausages, or on its own with some good bread.

Slice the cabbage into ½-inch wide strips and put it into a bowl. Add 1 teaspoon of salt and use your hands to massage it in well.

Heat the oil in a deep frying pan or shallow, flameproof casserole over medium-low heat. Add the onions, along with a pinch of salt to help release their juices and stop them from burning. You could also cover the onions with a lid or cartouche (cut out a circle of baking parchment about the same size as your pan, then wet it) to speed things up a bit. Cook, stirring every so often, until the onions are soft and turning a deep golden color. Add a splash of water if they seem dry or are starting to catch on the pan bottom a bit.

Now add the cabbage and caraway seeds and turn down the heat to low. Cover with a lid and cook for about 20 minutes, or until the cabbage starts softening. If it gets too dry, add a splash of water. Add the red bell pepper and cook for another 5 minutes.

Gently warm the tomato juice in a small pan, then stir in the crème fraîche and add to the cabbage. Taste the sauce and make sure it is well seasoned – otherwise the cabbage will be too bland and it will not become the cabbage of your dreams. Cover and braise for another 30-40 minutes – when it is ready, the cabbage should be soft, but not falling apart. Stir through the parsley and serve.

Beet tops

SERVES 4-6 AS A SIDE

---

14 oz beet leaves and stalks, well washed

1 Tbsp canola oil and/or
1 Tbsp butter

2 garlic cloves, finely chopped

Large handful of chopped dill, stalks and fronds kept separate

2 Tbsp crème fraîche or heavy cream

Sea salt and black pepper

Generously given to me by a contemporary food writer from Lviv, Marianna Dushar, this recipe has a rather devastating history. During hungry years in Ukraine, people survived on dishes such as this, along with similar, often foraged, plants like wild quinoa leaves (*lebeda*). It is important to remember one's history, and I think this might be one of the reasons why I hate waste so much. When you buy beets with the leaves attached, do not chuck them away – they taste like chard. If they look a little sad, let them sit in some ice-cold water for a few minutes to perk them up and then dry with a kitchen towel. This may be a simple-sounding dish, but it is very tasty.

Roughly chop the larger beet leaves, keeping any smaller ones whole. Finely chop the stalks, then blanch in a pan of boiling water for 1 minute. Rinse under cold running water to refresh, then drain.

Put the oil and/or butter into a large skillet or saucepan and set over medium-low heat. Add the beet leaves. Cover with a lid and cook for a few minutes, then take the lid off and give them a stir. When they start to wilt, stir in the garlic and chopped dill stalks and cook for a few more minutes, just so the garlic loses its harshness. Finally add the crème fraîche or cream and chopped dill fronds, then season well with salt and pepper.

Fried tomatoes with garlic and cheese

SERVES 4-6

---

2 Tbsp vegetable or olive oil

5 green or other firm tomatoes, cut in half crosswise

1 small garlic clove, crushed

4 oz ricotta salata or feta cheese

Sea salt

Bread, to serve

This is often made in southern Ukraine, close to the Moldovan border, once the sun starts fading in October. Traditionally, a sheep's milk cheese called *brynza* is used. In terms of texture and flavor, this lies somewhere between feta and ricotta salata, both of which work really well as substitutes. As for the tomatoes, firmer ones or green tomatoes are ideal. So if the tomatoes you grow do not quite ripen, try this! It is simple, but so delicious.

Heat the oil in a large frying pan over medium-high heat. When the oil is very hot, carefully place the tomato halves, skin side down, in the hot pan. As soon as you hear sizzling, cover with a lid (or improvise with a big plate or baking sheet). Cook the tomatoes for 2 minutes, then flip them over, cover again and cook for another 3 minutes. Flip them back on to their skin side and sprinkle with salt, then cook, uncovered, for a minute or two, to reduce and intensify any juices that have accumulated.

Lift the tomatoes out onto a plate and smudge a little crushed garlic over the cut sides. If there are any cooking juices left in the pan, pour these over the garlic to temper its rawness slightly.

Finally, using a fine grater, make it snow over the tomatoes – you might not need all the cheese, but I do like to use quite a lot if it's good! Eat scooped over some bread for breakfast or a light lunch.

Young garlic scapes in butter

SERVES 4 AS A SIDE

_____

14 oz garlic scapes

1 Tbsp olive or canola oil

2 Tbsp butter

Sea salt and black pepper

Garlic scapes are often left to go sour in a brine and eaten throughout winter as a pickle. But sometimes they are just fried, and butter seems to be a natural partner for them. You could also stir through some breadcrumbs for extra crunch. Served with boiled new potatoes, this is one of the tastiest things you can eat in the summer.

Cook the garlic scapes in salted boiling water for 5 minutes, then drain in a colander and refresh under cold running water. Cut the scapes into 2½-inch lengths.

When you're almost ready to serve, heat the oil and butter in a frying pan over medium heat and sizzle the scapes for about 5 minutes. Season to taste with salt and pepper, then serve.

Hutsul polenta

SERVES 4 (OR 2 HUTSUL
SHEPHERDS)

Ukrainian Hutsul people, from the highlands, have a very distinct regional cuisine that relies heavily on crops that do well in the mountains. Corn is one of them, hence their prolific use of ground corn, which is similar to polenta.

Most Hutsul dishes are very hearty. Life in the mountains is tough, with little time left for cooking after a hard day's work, and so meals need to be rustled up pretty quickly. This one, called *banosh*, was taught to me in a summer kitchen nestled in a hidden valley of the verdant Carpathian hills. There are many variations: *kulesha* is corn cooked in water and flavored with garlic, *yeshnytsya* is cooked in milk and enriched with egg, while *tokan* is a baked version.

Traditionally cooked outdoors over an open fire, a portion of this corn porridge would sustain a shepherd for many hours. *Banosh* is often served with some local cheese, either *brynza* (a salty sheep's milk cheese) or *vurda* (a kind of curd cheese). Make sure you use good-quality crème fraîche and cheese here – it will make all the difference.

If you have any left over, it will keep in the fridge for a couple of days. A good way of using it up is to flatten the cold *banosh* into a cake, then heat a little oil in a small frying pan and fry it over medium heat for 3 minutes or so until it forms a crust underneath.

1½ cups crème fraîche

1 heaping tsp sea salt

1¼ cups coarse polenta

Pinch of thyme leaves

Pinch of marjoram leaves –
optional

4 oz feta cheese, crumbled,
to serve

Put the crème fraîche and 1 cup of water into a heavy-based pan, add the salt, and bring to a simmer over medium heat.

Now slowly pour in the polenta, stirring all the time with a wooden spoon. Keep stirring for 15 minutes or so, as the *banosh* gets thicker and glossier. As soon as you see pools of butter collecting on the surface, stop cooking – it's done. The consistency should remain rather sloppy. Stir in the thyme and some marjoram, if you have it.

Serve your *banosh* with the cheese – it is very rich and makes a meal in itself.

Crushed potatoes with fava beans

SERVES 4

¾ lb baking potatoes, skins on

2 oz *salo* (page 338), *lardo,* or bacon

A little vegetable oil, if needed

1 small onion (or 4 green onions), thinly sliced

7 oz shelled fresh fava beans (from 1 lb unshelled)
or
5 oz (¾ cup) frozen fava beans

¼ cup crème fraîche

1 Tbsp chopped dill

Sea salt and black pepper

Crushed potatoes with fava beans and *salo* (cured pork fat) is another Hutsul staple, although versions of it are also found in western Belarus and Lithuania.

In spring and early summer, fresh fava beans and boiled new potatoes are used to make this dish; in the colder months, frozen fava beans and baked potato flesh make a good alternative. Crispy nubs of pork fat add an extra luxurious flavor. However, traditionally *salo* would not have been used during Lent, so feel free to stick to green onions if you prefer, or if you are vegetarian.

Preheat the oven to 400°F. Bake the potatoes for 45 minutes–1 hour – you are aiming for soft, perfectly baked potatoes.

Meanwhile, heat the *salo, lardo,* or bacon in a frying pan over a medium-low heat until it starts to release its fat. Add a splash of oil if you're using bacon and you feel it needs a little help. Then, when it starts to get crisp, add the onion and cook for a few minutes to soften.

Cook the fava beans in a pan of salted boiling water for about 5 minutes, then drain.

Scoop the warm potato flesh out of the skins and put it into a saucepan over a very low heat. (The skins would be fed to animals, but do not throw them out even if you lack a pigsty – just keep them in the fridge and use to flavor your next vegetable stock.) Add the beans to the potatoes and crush until fairly smooth, but still with some texture. Stir in the crème fraîche and dill, then season generously with salt and pepper.

Spoon the *salo, lardo,* or bacon, together with its fat, over the dish and serve right away.

Potato cakes stuffed with bean and feta paste

SERVES 2–3 AS A STARTER
(MAKES 6 POTATO CAKES)

BEAN AND FETA PASTE

1 Tbsp vegetable oil

1 small onion, finely diced

7 oz canned cannellini beans
(half a 15-oz can), drained

4 oz feta cheese, crumbled

Handful of finely chopped dill

GARLIC YOGURT

½ cup + 2 Tbsp yogurt

1 small garlic clove, crushed

1¾ lb russet potatoes, peeled

1 onion, peeled

1 egg, lightly beaten

About 6 Tbsp all-purpose flour

Scant 1 tsp fast-action
dried yeast

2 Tbsp vegetable oil

Sea salt and black pepper

Chile paste (page 59), to serve

Potato cakes are made all over Ukraine, with endless variations in each region – but it was right by the Belarus border that I encountered the most delicious ones. These rather unusual yeast-leavened potato cakes were being cooked over a *pich* stove in a small village called Urdyutsk. I was shown how they could be stuffed with either salted herby curd cheese or bean paste. I couldn't decide which version to give you, so I combined the two!

If you want to make this recipe vegan, collect the starchy water squeezed out of the grated potato and onion in a bowl. Carefully pour off the liquid to leave the starch behind and use this to bind the potato cakes instead of the egg.

For the bean and feta paste, heat the oil in a frying pan over medium heat. Add the diced onion and a pinch of salt and cook until golden. Mash the beans and feta to a smooth paste, then mix in the onion and set aside for later.

For the garlic yogurt, simply mix the ingredients in a small bowl.

Grate the potatoes on the fine side of a box grater, then grate the onion on the coarse side. Put the grated potato and onion into a fine sieve set over a bowl and squeeze out some, but not all of the liquid, reserving it in the bowl.

Put the sloppy potato and onion mix into another bowl and stir in the egg, flour, and yeast. Leave somewhere warm for at least 10 minutes, until slightly bubbly, then season with salt and pepper. The mixture should be the consistency of thick pancake batter – add some more flour if it seems too thin, or a little of the reserved potato liquid if it feels too thick.

Now heat the oil in a large frying pan over medium-low heat. Moving quite swiftly, drop tablespoonfuls of the potato mixture into the pan, using the back of the spoon to spread out into circles about 4 inches in diameter. You should be able to cook about three at a time, but take care not to overcrowd the pan.

As soon as they are in the pan, spoon some bean and feta paste onto each potato cake, then place another, smaller spoonful of the raw potato mixture on top, spreading it over the paste to seal. When the underside of the potato cakes is golden, carefully turn them, one by one, and cook on the other side for 2–3 minutes. You may need to flip them again and cook for another few minutes on each side to make sure they are hot right through.

Serve with the garlic yogurt and a dab of chile paste.

Meat and fish

FROM PASTURE, RIVER, AND SEA

My grandparents kept animals: a cow called Maya, for her milk, and a couple of goats, again for the milk and eventually for meat. Wiry cockerels and chickens, resembling their dinosaur ancestors, would be dispatched once they reached the ripe old age of four, their meat tough but extremely flavorsome.

As in the rest of peasant Europe, pigs would be slaughtered before Christmas, when the weather was cold enough that their meat wouldn't spoil before it could be preserved and stored. The offal would be eaten on the same day, stuffed inside yeasted buns called *pyrizhky*, and the blood used to make *krovyanka* sausage.

The remarkable *zinkivska* sausage comes from the Vinnytsia region, where my paternal grandfather was born. The sausage casings are filled with hand-chopped meat, *salo* (cured pork fat), garlic, and seasoning, before being brushed with blood. The sausage is then smoked over fruit wood and basted with blood over and over again. Its flavor is unique – smoky and rich from its blood lacquer – and the whole process could easily take a whole day.

Over the centuries, the territory of Ukraine has been subject to many raids by Muslim conquerors from the north and east, and during these incursions, most livestock apart from pigs would have been taken away. This is probably one of the reasons why pork became such a popular and revered meat – ribs, knuckles, trotters, tails, and ears, everything would have been eaten.

This kind of nose-to-tail eating applied to every animal – I even came across an old recipe from Odesa using elders (cow's udders). I discovered that these were also eaten in the UK until relatively recently, but they seem to have fallen out of favor these days and I could not find them anywhere. Happily, I had more luck with ox tongue and so have included a recipe for braised tongue, which is a surprisingly versatile thing to have in the fridge.

Fish feature in many local dishes along the coastlines of the Sea of Azov and the Black Sea, especially in the port of Odesa, where people really know their way round the preparation and cooking of fish. In a country threaded by rivers, freshwater fish such as pike, carp, and zander often make an appearance too. Do feel free to substitute your favorite fish in the recipes given here, and please be guided by the latest sustainability ratings – these change frequently, depending on stock levels of the various fisheries.

On *pich*

Long before kerosene and gas stoves became popular in Ukraine, there was an oven that was more than an oven. Called *pich* in Ukrainian, this substantial masonry oven would be built into the structure of a house. A proper *pich* would be crafted by an expert mason, a trade that has almost died out now – you had to sign up well in advance for your *pich* to be built and wait your turn. Such an oven also featured in some summer kitchens, especially those that were originally used as interim accommodation while the main house was being constructed.

It is believed that masonry ovens date back to Kyivan Rus, and examples survive in Russia, Belarus, and other Eastern European countries. Russian Old Believers in southwest Ukraine build a similar outdoor oven under an awning, which is known as *garnushka* ("the lovely one"), and in other parts of Ukraine these outside ovens are called *kabytsya*.

Those who did not abandon or destroy their traditional oven still reap the benefits. The clay construction was designed to retain heat for many hours, making it very economical and helping to eke out the supply of wood logs or hay that was used for both heating and cooking. In places near rivers, such as Vylkove, reeds were used to fire up the *pich*, and in areas where corn grew well, this would be dried and used as fuel. Apart from the main oven, there were also usually a few alcoves that served as warming ovens – these were where my grandmother would lay out sunflower seeds to slowly toast, or mushrooms and herbs to dry. Traditionally, cast-iron and clay pots were used to cook in the *pich*. These were shaped like an amphora: the small circumference of the base meant food wouldn't catch and burn, the bulbous middle section guaranteed even heating from all sides, and the narrow neck minimized evaporation, keeping in nutrients and flavor.

>>

Being multifunctional, the *pich* was also used for drying clothes, and even for washing by households without a sauna. There was usually a sleeping bench (*lizhanka*) or two in the *pich*, often with a special hatch in which hay could be lit to gently warm the occupants. But the *pich* went beyond being functional: its pivotal role in cooking and the life of a family made it almost sacred, with a cultlike status. It might be decorated with beautifully painted ornate flowers and intricate patterns – in the belief that these motifs would distract or even trap evil spirits in their many whorls.

Often the oven would be spoken of in anthropomorphic terms, usually as if it were a mother; it may even have been given a name and addressed directly. It was considered extremely bad manners to swear in front of the *pich* – in fact, there is a Ukrainian expression that roughly translates as, "I would tell you (where to go), but there is a *pich* in the house.'

Similarly, quarreling near your *pich* was frowned upon, as the oven was perceived to be a source of all things positive and life-giving. Women even gave birth on top of their *pich*. There was another tradition (luckily in the past now!) where, before a young woman left her parents' house to be married, she would scratch at the oven's whitewashed surfaces, so that bits of the *pich* – and symbolically her family and home – would remain with her, under her nails.

It was also thought that the *pich* had healing powers. Many of my grandparents' generation remember coming home from school, often a long and arduous walk in flimsy shoes and sodden socks, to climb on top of the *pich*, where they would bury icicle-like feet into the warmth of drying meadow grasses, barley, oat hay, and wild herbs. They insist that they were never ill as children because the warmth of the oven and the essential oils from the herbs kept them well.

Pretty much every minority in Ukraine used these ovens, so just like the summer kitchen itself, the *pich* was something that created common ground and united people – for instance, Jewish people in Besarabia might ask their non-Jewish Ukrainian neighbors to come over and light their ovens for them on the Sabbath. The *pich* was irreplaceable during fasting, when you couldn't use oil or fats to cook. In Vylkove, by the Danube River, a dish called *pekanka* used to be made: a lot of salt was placed inside the *pich* and then small fish were placed on top and baked until tender and fragrant. This would be served with *salamur* (a garlic and herb paste tempered with a little hot broth), baked potatoes, and pickles.

Nadezhda (Nadya) Kovardiuk, from Lyshnynka village, in the northwestern marshes of Ukraine, now lives in her summer kitchen, which has been turned into a "granny flat." There is even a bath there, right by the *pich* oven, and she has many fond memories of the beloved *pich*: "Wood would be stacked tic-tac-toe and left to burn for a while. To test if it was ready, we would throw in a little flour and if it burnt immediately, the fire was ready." The *pich* was used a lot to preserve things for the winter: meat was slowly cooked in large clay or enamel pots, then covered with lard and kept in the *lyoh*, a rough dugout cellar in the ground. If the meat was perfectly seasoned, it would be eaten with a little bread for lunch. If someone had been a little heavy-handed and it came out too salty, it would be used in small quantities as a seasoning, mixed through some boiled potatoes or grains. The "clean fat" on top of *tushonka* (preserved pork) was melted down and strained, ready to be used for cooking. Nothing was wasted.

In Opishnya, in central Ukraine, I sat in a summer kitchen with seven women. The oldest was just over ninety, and her daughter, in her fifties, pointed to a gas stove in the corner of the kitchen, lamenting that she no longer knew how to light, clean, and maintain a *pich*. But she did remember how her mum used to preserve local plums, one of the most fascinating methods I have ever come across. Some ripe plums would be packed into a large clay pot and put into the fading warmth of a *pich* that had done its work for the day. In the morning, the juices would be drained off and some fresh plums would be added on top of

>>

the sunken cooked plums. They would repeat this process at the end of each day for a week, until the plums filled the clay pot to the rim. The final layer of fresh plums would be added and baked at a higher temperature, until they caramelized to create a natural sugary seal. Plums preserved in their own concentrated juice, with a self-sealing plum lid, struck me as a pinnacle of preserving ingenuity.

I have seen a lot of *pich* ovens all over Ukraine, both in main houses and summer kitchens. Nadya's children, who have built their new house a short distance away from her summer-kitchen-turned-granny-flat, have also built a *pich* and are planning to use it to warm their house and for cooking. So there is hope that, with the renewed interest in the traditional ways, Ukrainians will continue to restore or build – and use – these ancient and wondrous ovens.

Pot-roast chicken cooked in herby crème fraîche

SERVES 6

½ cup + 2 Tbsp crème fraîche

6 Tbsp dill and/or parsley or their stalks, roughly chopped

4 garlic cloves, roughly chopped

1 Tbsp canola oil

1 whole chicken, about 3 lb

Sea salt and black pepper

Chicken smothered and baked in cultured cream is an old classic, but sometimes I like to go one step further. I use a lot of herbs at home, and sometimes I am left with quite a few stalks: dill, parsley, basil, and cilantro stalks all work well when stirred into the crème fraîche. By the time the chicken is cooked, this turns into the most amazing sauce.

I like serving this with chunks of good bread and boiled cabbage or the cabbage and cucumber salad on page 214, but it would also be lovely with new potatoes or a buttery lemon rice pilaf. Any leftovers are delicious stirred through hot stubby pasta.

Blitz the crème fraîche, herbs, garlic, and a generous pinch of salt in a food processor until smooth. Taste, and add more salt if needed, and some pepper.

Pour the oil into a roasting pan, add the chicken and spread the herby crème fraîche all over it, inside and out. If you have time, cover and leave to marinate for a couple of hours at room temperature, or in the fridge overnight.

Preheat the oven to 400°F.

Cover the chicken loosely with foil and roast for 45 minutes, basting it a couple of times, if you remember. Take off the foil and cook for another 15–20 minutes, or until the legs come away from the body with ease and the juices run clear from the thickest part of the thigh when it is pierced with the tip of a knife.

Take the chicken out of the oven and let it rest for 5–10 minutes. Pull the tender meat from the bones with two forks and mix through the roasting juices, then serve.

Sour cabbage leaf rolls with pork and barley

SERVES 4

My grandmother Lyusia would make cabbage rolls for my mum when she was little, but for some reason she'd stopped making them by the time we came along, so for me this dish has always had a bit of a legendary feel to it. The original involved small hand-cut bits of pork belly mixed with onion and rice, all neatly wrapped in brine-fermented cabbage leaves, then cooked in a sour cream sauce. I recreated my grandma's dish from my mum's description and then I made the following variation, using shreds of meat and garlic with barley. This is a good way to use up any leftover slow-roast pork (or other tender meat, such as confit duck). Even better if you had the meat with a grain, like freekeh or rice – just mix the leftovers together and use as the filling.

The women at the pickle stalls in the market used to always have whole leaves at the bottom of the sauerkraut barrel, so once the kraut was all sold, these prized leaves would be snatched up to make cabbage rolls. Make sure you use well-fermented cabbage leaves too, so they'll be soft and pliable for rolling (or you could use blanched fresh cabbage leaves).

6 Tbsp pearl barley

½ lb slow-roast pork (page 262), pulled into shreds or finely chopped

8 oz (1½ cups) cooked chestnuts, finely chopped

1 Tbsp vegetable oil

3½ Tbsp butter

10 large garlic cloves, thinly sliced

1 cup crème fraîche

¾ cup chicken stock, mushroom stock, or water

8 whole cabbage leaves from sauerkraut (page 28), cut in half

Sea salt and black pepper

Fresh bread, to serve

Put the pearl barley into a pan of cold salted water and bring to a boil, then turn down to a simmer and cook for 20–30 minutes, or until just cooked. Drain, tip into a bowl, and leave to cool. Add the pork and chestnuts to the barley and season with salt and pepper, then mush it all together into a homogenous mass.

Now for the sauce. First of all, do not be alarmed at the amount of garlic – we will cook it slowly until it is mellow. Heat the oil and butter in a small cast-iron casserole or saucepan over low heat and, when it foams, add the garlic. Cook, stirring from time to time, until you get that heady smell of confit garlic. Watch it closely – you don't want it to brown at all. In a small bowl, whisk the crème fraîche with the stock or water and add to the pan, then remove from the heat and set aside.

Preheat the oven to 400°F. Take your cabbage leaves and cut out any tougher bits of stalk. Lay a leaf on your worktop and put a tablespoonful of the pork and barley filling close to the stalk end, then flip the bottom of the leaf up and over the filling. Fold in the sides and roll up as tightly as possible, leaving the finished roll on the worktop, seam side down. Repeat with the rest of the cabbage leaves and filling.

Carefully lower the rolls, seam side down, into a baking dish, nestling them in a single layer. Pour over the sauce, cover, and bake for 15 minutes, then take off the lid and bake for 10 more minutes. Serve with bread.

Sashko's *bogracz* stew

SERVES 6–8

There are versions of *bogracz* stew in all parts of the former Austro-Hungarian Empire, including what is now Transcarpathian Ukraine. It is an incredible dish, one for the real meat-lover. The name *bogracz* refers to the cauldron-like cast-iron pot that was traditionally used to cook the stew over the fire. This version comes from a village near Mukacheve, close to the border with Hungary, and was given to me by Sashko Lipchey. Apart from sharing great recipes, Sashko does amazing things for the community, such as his "gift a cow" project, where a family is given a calf, on condition that when the calf grows up and has its own calf, they must pass it on to a neighbor, and so on.

Most people in western Ukraine buy the spice mix for *bogracz* at the market. I bought some too and spied the ingredients list, so now you can make your own – everything is easy enough to get hold of! This recipe uses three types of meat and an array of pork products, and the result is outstanding. Feel free to use just lamb ribs, but do try to find a slab of good pancetta or smoked bacon: it adds so much flavor, especially if you're cooking this on the stove top and not over a fire outside – although making *bogracz* is a great excuse for a cook-out.

SPICE MIX

2 bay leaves

2 Tbsp juniper berries

1 Tbsp sesame seeds

4 tsp black peppercorns

1 Tbsp caraway seeds

1 Tbsp dried marjoram

1 Tbsp dried oregano

1 Tbsp garlic powder

1 Tbsp smoked paprika

¼ nutmeg, freshly grated

For the spice mix, crumble or tear the bay leaves and blitz to a powder with the rest of the ingredients in a spice or coffee grinder. It will keep in an airtight container for a couple of months.

Peel the onions for the stew, then dice three of them, but leave the rest whole. Put a little oil into a heavy-based pot over medium-low heat and add the pancetta or smoked pork belly. Cook until golden all over – if it starts to stick, add a splash of water and scrape the base of the pot with a wooden spoon.

Add the diced onions and carrots, along with a pinch of salt to help them release moisture, and cook, stirring from time to time, until they soften and start to turn golden. If the pot starts looking dry, add a splash of water. Stir in the sweet paprika and cook for a few minutes, then tip everything into a bowl and set aside. At this point hungry Transcarpathians would dip in a piece of bread and eat it as an impromptu snack!

Add a tablespoon of oil to the same pot (no need to wash it), add the ribs, and cook over medium heat, turning from time to time, for 5–10 minutes, or until the meat becomes golden-cheeked. Now add the chile paste and 2 tablespoons of the spice mix and cook, stirring, for 2 minutes.

STEW

5 onions

Canola oil

9-oz slab of pancetta or smoked pork belly, cut into ¾-inch cubes

½ lb carrots, scrubbed and diced

1 Tbsp sweet paprika

1 lb beef or lamb ribs

1½ lb pork ribs

1 Tbsp chile paste (page 59)

14.5 oz canned tomatoes (or fresh, ripe ones)

14 oz jarred red bell peppers
or
2 large red bell peppers

1 red chile, bruised – optional

6 small potatoes, scrubbed and cut into chunks

3 large garlic cloves, finely chopped

Handful of chopped parsley

Handful of chopped dill

Handful of thinly sliced green onions – optional

Sea salt

Crusty bread, to serve

Pour enough cold water into the pot to just cover the meat (around 1½–2 quarts), season with salt, and return the onions, carrots, and pancetta or pork belly to the pot. Bring to a boil, then turn down the heat as low as it will go and simmer gently for 1 hour – covered, but with a little gap for the steam to escape.

Now add the whole onions, tomatoes, and peppers – and the chile, if using. Simmer for another hour or until the meat starts falling apart. The tomatoes and peppers will almost disintegrate and become part of the sauce, but the onions should remain pretty much whole – and for some it's these onions saturated with all the meat juices and spices that are the best part of the *bogracz*. Add the potatoes and cook for 10–15 minutes, or until the potatoes are soft but not falling apart.

Finally, stir in the garlic, herbs, and green onions, if using. You will need some crusty bread with this to mop up the delicious juices. The whole vegetables are a special treat!

Slow-roast pork with kraut and dried fruit

SERVES 6

There are many interpretations of this slow-roast pork, which is eaten all over Ukraine and along its borders – this one is a bit like a dandy version of Polish *bigos*, with the tender meat and aromatic kraut sweetened with apples, prunes, and apricots.

Sometimes when I cook this pork, I have to almost forcibly prevent my family from polishing it off, just so I can use the leftovers as a filling for the brioche-like buns called *pyrizhky*. The first time I tried this mind-blowing combination was one Christmas at home in Ukraine. As usual I had arrived late, after the twelve-hour rickety train from Kyiv to Kherson, and my mum gave me a sweet, soft bun filled with pork, kraut, and dried fruit. It was the best thing I had ever eaten! I implore you to save some of this for the buns on page 164 – or just buy some good-quality brioche buns and stuff the leftovers into those, along with a handful of watercress.

SPICE RUB

2 tsp sea salt

5 large garlic cloves, crushed

3 Tbsp Dijon mustard

3 Tbsp cider vinegar

¼ nutmeg, grated

1 tsp honey

5½ lb pork belly, shoulder or knuckle (hock)

1 tsp olive or vegetable oil

1 large onion, thickly sliced

1 lb sauerkraut, drained

4 oz prunes, pitted and roughly chopped

2–4 oz dried apricots, thickly sliced

2 tsp caraway seeds, lightly toasted and ground

2 tsp coriander seeds, lightly toasted and ground

2 tsp fennel seeds, lightly toasted and ground

1 lb apples, cored and thinly sliced

For the spice rub, mix all of the ingredients together. Rub all over the pork and leave to marinate, covered, for as long as you can spare – up to a couple of hours at room temperature, or overnight in the fridge.

Preheat the oven to 400°F. Line a roasting pan with foil and place a rack in it. Place the pork on the rack and roast for 15–20 minutes, then turn the oven down to 325°F and cook for 1 hour.

Heat the oil in a large frying pan and fry the onion until starting to color. Add the sauerkraut, dried fruit, caraway, coriander, and fennel and cook for 5 minutes, then stir through the apples.

Remove the pork from the oven and carefully lift the pork on its rack off the roasting pan. Tip the contents of the frying pan into the roasting pan and sit the pork directly on top. Cover with foil and return to the oven for a further 2 hours.

Remove from the oven and let it rest for 10–15 minutes. Slice the pork (or pull it into shreds) and serve on top of the kraut and fruit.

Lyusia's goat and onion stew with creamy mash

SERVES 4

My grandmother Lyusia had a penchant for eccentric pet and livestock names. Her cat was called Nero, and he really was both lascivious and slightly tyrannical. Her two sweet, innocent goats, however, went by the names of Shevardnadze (so-called because of its curly gray hair) and Hussein (for its black curls). I'm not sure which one was sacrificed for the pot first, but maybe naming them after politicians made it easier to dispatch them.

She mainly kept goats for milking. But the females would have kids once a year, and the male kids were destined for the pot. When the time came, the whole family feasted for days – it was a real celebration. With the bony parts, Lyusia made *tuzluk* (similar to the spring lamb broth, or *shurpa*, on page 130). The legs and shoulders were made into a simple stew with lots of onions, to be eaten with a different side dish over a couple of days. This is very good served with pickles, sauerkraut, or even kimchi. For me, nothing beats a combination of strong gherkins and soothing mash.

2 Tbsp vegetable oil

1½ lb goat leg steaks
(or shoulder meat)

3 cups thickly sliced onions

2 bay leaves

Sea salt and black pepper

Quick-fermented cucumbers
(page 26) or pickles, to serve

MASH

1 lb russet potatoes, peeled and
cut into chunks

2 cups whole milk

1 egg yolk

3–5 Tbsp butter

Heat the oil in a heavy-based pot over medium-high heat. Add the goat, in batches, being careful not to overcrowd the pot, and brown well on all sides – the key to this is to give the meat a bit of time on each side, without moving it too much. Put the browned meat on a plate and set aside.

Add the onions to the same pot, scraping up any caramelized bits from the base of the pot. Turn down the heat to medium-low and cook, stirring from time to time, until the onions soften and start coloring a little. If the pot looks a little dry or there are crusty bits sticking to it, add a splash of water and scrape the base with a wooden spoon. Now return the goat to the pot and add the bay leaves. Season well with salt and pepper, then pour in enough water to cover the meat. Cover the pot with a lid or cartouche (cut out a circle of baking parchment about the same size as your pan, then wet it), turn down the heat as low as possible, and cook for about an hour, or until the meat is soft and falling apart, adding a touch more water if it starts looking dry.

Meanwhile, for the mash, put the potatoes and milk into a saucepan and bring to a boil, then turn down to a simmer - do keep an eye on the pan, as milk has a tendency to foam up and run out of the pan! Cook for 30 minutes, or until the potatoes are very soft. Drain the potatoes over a large bowl, reserving the milk. Mash the potatoes until very smooth (or use a food mill), then add the egg yolk, butter, and a splash of the reserved milk. Keep adding the milk until you reach the consistency you enjoy - I like my mash to be quite sloppy. Check for seasoning and add more salt or pepper, if you like. Serve the goat stew on top of the mash, with some punchy pickles on the side.

Ukrainian blood sausage

MAKES 2 X 14-OZ
SAUSAGES

This soft, tasty sausage is eaten all over Ukraine, and when I moved to the UK I was pleasantly surprised to find blood pudding on the breakfast menu. It reminded me of the blood sausage I'd had at home in Ukraine, but often it was a lot drier. Two things make the Ukrainian version so luscious: the unapologetically huge amount of cream that goes into it; and the use of fresh blood, which makes for a far superior sausage.

Unfortunately, it is almost impossible to find fresh pig's blood in the UK, so I decided to give a recipe for the dried stuff (suppliers of this – and sausage casings – are listed on pages 340–1). If you are able to source fresh pig's blood, you'll need a quart; if it has become clumpy, you'll need to blitz it in a food processor before using it. You'll also need a thermometer and a funnel. If this is your first time making blood pudding or sausages, make sure you have all your ingredients weighed out and prepped before you start – and, ideally, a friend to share the experience with!

2 x 3-foot lengths of pork sausage casings

1¼ cup (200g) buckwheat

7 oz dried pig's blood

1 cup heavy cream

1¼ cups (150g) all-purpose flour

1¾ cups diced onion

7 oz *salo* (page 338), *lardo,* or smoked pancetta, finely diced (freezing it prior helps)

1 Tbsp sea salt

2 tsp freshly ground black or white pepper

Bread and pickles, to serve

Soak the sausage casings in cold water for about 2 hours.

Cook the buckwheat in boiling water for about 7 minutes, until half-cooked. Drain well, then leave to cool.

In a large saucepan, warm 3 cups of water to 105°F (just warm to the touch), then whisk in the blood. In another saucepan, warm up the cream to the same temperature, then whisk in the flour – if the mixture looks clumpy, pass it through a sieve. Next stir the cream mixture into the blood, along with the buckwheat, onion, *salo, lardo,* or pancetta, and salt and pepper.

Now for the fun part. Do not worry too much about the casing – it is much more resilient than you might think. However, do have a large bowl or deep tray ready to catch the mixture, in case disaster strikes! Drain the casings, then make a couple of tight knots at one end of each length. Take one of the casings and roll the open end over the spout of the funnel, holding it firmly in place. Ladle the blood sausage mixture into a jug and then slowly pour it into the funnel; if it gets stuck, push it through with the handle of a wooden spoon. This might all feel a little peculiar – but embrace it, the results will be well worth it!

Keep going until you've used up about half the mixture and the casing is almost full, leaving just enough casing for you to tie two knots at the other end. Gently curl the sausage and set it aside. Now repeat the process with the other casing and the rest of the mixture.

Fill a large, deep stockpot or pan with water and bring it to 150°F (barely simmering), then gently lower the blood sausages into the hot water. After 5 minutes or so, prick each sausage in a few places with a needle and continue to cook for about 30 minutes, keeping the water at the same temperature. Drain the sausages and let them cool. They will keep for 5 days in the fridge, and they freeze well too.

When you want to serve them, heat some oil in a large frying pan and fry the blood sausage – either a whole curl or some chunks of it – until crisp on both sides and warmed all the way through. Eat with bread and pickles.

Braised ox tongue

SERVES 8-10

---

2 lb ox tongue

1 onion, halved

2 carrots, scrubbed and roughly chopped

2 celery ribs, roughly chopped

2 bay leaves

Sea salt

I grew up in a culture where eating offal was a regular thing. Light broths would often be made with poultry necks, hearts, and gizzards, and quite often there would be tongue in the fridge. When I first came to the UK, it seemed strange to me that offal was not more widely used. Yes, some people might have eaten liver or kidneys, but many did not even know what gizzards were. Now my British husband tells me that he remembers there being ox tongue in the fridge when he was a kid in the 1980s.

I love the texture and flavor of ox tongue – and, for comparatively little money, you can buy enough to last you for a few days. In Ukraine it is eaten cold, cut into thick slices, and it makes great sandwiches, with crème fraîche or mayonnaise flavored with horseradish (page 108) or dill and garlic (page 192). You can also use it in a potato and pea salad with a mustardy creamy dressing, or fry it in a little oil until crisp, then serve it with salsa verde.

If you have the time, you can brine the tongue, so it will become more tender and flavorful when cooked. Simply mix 5 tablespoons of sea salt into 2 quarts of water, making sure it dissolves completely. Cover the tongue with the cold brine and leave in the fridge for about 8 hours or overnight, then drain and rinse.

But often I don't bother with the brining and just braise it in the following manner. Put the ox tongue into a large stockpot and cover with cold water. Add all the vegetables, along with the bay leaves and a pinch of salt (if the tongue has not been previously brined). Bring to a boil, skimming off the foamy gray froth from the surface, then lower the heat to a gentle simmer.

The tongue will take 3–4 hours to cook, but all you have to do is keep the water topped up so the tongue is completely covered. You can use cold water for topping up – this will bring more impurities to the surface for you to skim. At the start of cooking, the tongue will seize up and look very hard and rigid, but it will slowly relax as it cooks. When it is soft (test by piercing it with a small knife), briefly rinse under cold running water and, when it is cool enough to handle, peel off the top layer.

The braised tongue will keep in your fridge for a week or so, or for up to 3 months in the freezer. The stock is good enough to be used to make borsch or a Southeast Asian broth, or in a winter stew, and you can always reduce it and then freeze it for another day.

Pig's ears with garlic and paprika

SERVES 6 AS A SNACK

---

6 pig's ears

2 leeks, roughly chopped

2 celery ribs, roughly chopped

1 carrot, scrubbed and roughly chopped

1 onion, peeled but left whole

2–5 garlic cloves (to taste), peeled but left whole

1 tsp sweet paprika

1 tsp hot or smoked paprika

Sea salt

I start salivating just at the thought of this dish. I just love the cartilage and the skin rubbed in garlic and paprika paste – it is a real taste of my homeland.

When I offered these pig's ears to my son, Chinese food aficionado that he is, he declared, "This tastes like duck tongues! I like it, yes." I agree with him, I could eat a whole pig's ear by myself, especially if it is served with rye bread spread with beet and horseradish (page 61) – and maybe a beer or some ice-cold vodka.

Singe the hairs off the ears – I do this by holding them directly over the flame on my gas burner, being very careful of my sleeves! Trim off any fatty bits from the bottom of the ears, but do not throw the fat away: rub salt all over it and leave it in the fridge overnight, then wash the salt off, cut the cured fat into pieces, and use it for frying eggs.

Put the ears into a stockpot and cover with cold water. Bring to a boil, then drain, cover with fresh water (at least 2 quarts), and add the leeks, celery, carrot, and onion. Bring to a boil, then turn down to a simmer and cook for 1–1½ hours, until the pig's ears can be easily sliced through with a knife.

Meanwhile, use a mortar and pestle to crush the garlic to a paste with 2 teaspoons of salt, then mix in both paprikas. (Sometimes I use some of the chile paste on page 59 instead of the paprikas.)

Take the ears out of the broth, but do not throw it away – let it cool down and then freeze until you are ready to make a bowl of delicious ramen, or perhaps a meaty version of the mushroom broth with sour pickles on page 144.

Put the whole ears into a container that you have a lid for. Rub the garlic and paprika paste over the ears and cover with the lid. Let them cool down and then slice thinly.

Odesan confit sprats

MAKES ENOUGH TO FILL
A 16-OZ JAR

---

1 lb sprats or whitebait

1¾ cups onions thinly sliced
into circles

2–3 carrots, scrubbed and
cut into rounds

1 Tbsp black peppercorns

¾ cup good-quality sunflower
or mild olive oil

Sea salt

Rye bread and finely shredded
green onions, to serve

In Odesa, people really know their way around small fish. For this rich confit, they use the European sprat, *Sprattus sprattus*, and the end result has the same luscious quality as excellent canned fish.

This feels gruesome to write, but here goes: unless the fishmonger has already prepared your fish for you, gut them by ripping the head off and pulling downwards, taking the guts out at the same time. Either way, rinse the fish thoroughly and pat dry.

Put a layer of fish, side by side, into a small heavy-based pan. Sprinkle with salt, then add a layer of onions and carrots. Scatter over some of the peppercorns. Repeat these layers until all the fish, onions, carrots, and peppercorns are in the pan, then pour in the oil. It may seem like there isn't enough oil to cover everything, but the fish and vegetables will release liquid as they cook, so don't worry.

Set the pan over medium heat and wait until the oil starts to bubble gently, then turn down the heat as low as possible, so the oil is simmering ever so slightly. Cook the fish for about 1–1½ hours, or until soft and falling apart, then leave to cool. (You could also cook the sprats, covered, in a 325–350°F oven for the same length of time.)

You can store the confit sprats in a 16-ounce jar in the fridge for a week or more, as long as you make sure they are covered in oil.

To serve, spread on some rye bread and sprinkle with finely shredded green onions. (You can use the tasty oil in other fish recipes or for making fishy pasta sauces.)

Odesan sprats in batter

SERVES 2-4 AS A SNACK

---

20 sprats, gutted and butterflied

1 egg, beaten

½ cup whole milk

6 Tbsp (50g) all-purpose flour

¼–½ cup vegetable oil

Sea salt and black pepper

Lemon wedges, to serve

These battered sprats define Odesa for me. My namesake friend Olia made them in her flat in Odesa, after painstakingly cleaning every single tiny fish. It takes love, if you are in Ukraine. If you are elsewhere, by all means ask your fishmonger to help out! Her commentary, while she was cooking, was full of humor and communicative sounds. Picking up four little fish by their tails, they went "shookh, shookh" through the batter and then "pykh, pykh" into the hot oil. Soon we were sharing mutual "mniam, mniams" – and many memories of Ostap Bender, Odesa's most famous fictional con man, who appears in *The Twelve Chairs*, by Ilya Ilf and Yevgeniy Petrov, and is known for his healthy appetite.

Have the fish ready, all lined up tail to tail.

In a bowl, whisk the egg and milk together, then gradually add the flour bit by bit, whisking constantly, until you have a smooth batter the consistency of heavy cream. If it seems too thick or too thin, add a little water or flour respectively. Season the batter with salt and pepper.

Heat a ½-inch depth of oil in a frying pan over medium heat until a piece of bread thrown into it sizzles immediately. Pick up two fish by the tips of their tails and drag them through the batter, then gently lower them into the pan. Repeat with as many fish as the pan will hold, being careful not to overcrowd them. Cook on the first side for a minute, then turn and cook on the other side for 30 seconds. Lift out of the pan with a slotted spoon and drain on paper towels. Repeat until all the fish are cooked.

Serve with a squeeze of lemon – and a cold beer!

Panfried turbot

SERVES 2

---

2 turbot or flounder steaks

6 Tbsp all-purpose flour

2 Tbsp vegetable oil

Sea salt and white pepper

Panfried fish is a delicacy that's very typical of Odesa, and it's my mum's favorite dish. There, flounder would normally be cooked in this way, but it can be hard to find in the UK, so I often use turbot or dover sole instead as a treat, usually when my mum comes over to visit. The meat of turbot is sweet, and the gelatinous bits are so satisfying – I like to think of it as the oxtail of the sea. Serve this with a crunchy salad, such as the raw turnip and green onion one on page 204, or the cabbage and cucumber on page 214.

Lightly sprinkle salt all over your fish, then leave it for 10 minutes.

Scatter the flour over a plate and season with salt and pepper.

Heat the oil in a large frying pan, for which you have a lid, over medium heat. Dip each fish steak into the seasoned flour, shaking off any excess, then gently lower into the pan. Cover with the lid and steam-fry for 2 minutes, then flip it over and cook for another minute with the lid off. Drain on paper towels, then serve immediately.

Fishballs in tomato sauce

SERVES 2
(MAKES 10 FISHBALLS)

TOMATO SAUCE

1 Tbsp canola oil

1 small onion, finely diced

1 bay leaf

2 Tbsp tomato paste

1 x 14.5-oz can of diced tomatoes

2 Tbsp crème fraîche

1 small onion, roughly chopped

1 garlic clove, roughly chopped

10 oz fillet of pollack or similar

1–2 Tbsp fine semolina

A little beaten egg – optional

2 Tbsp canola or vegetable oil

Sea salt and black pepper

I grew up eating a lot of river fish – which, back then, I found just a bit too overpowering. Those same fish, however, were more than palatable in the fishballs my mum made. Full of magical childhood flavors, they are now, luckily, also enjoyed by my son, especially when they come with mash. They are also pretty good in a lunchbox, at room temperature over some couscous.

I always felt there was something quite Nordic about fishballs – perhaps there was mention of fish *frikadellen* in Tove Jansson's Moomin stories or Astrid Lindgren's "Karlsson on the Roof" books, I cannot recall. But when I eat these, I always think of being hygge-warm in my childhood home, reading and eating – still my favorite pastimes to this day.

First make the tomato sauce. Heat the oil in a saucepan over medium heat, then add the onion and a pinch of salt and cook, stirring, until translucent and just starting to turn golden. Add the bay leaf and tomato paste and cook for a minute or so, then add the canned tomatoes and season with salt and pepper. (My mum also adds a pinch of sugar, but I don't.) Let the sauce reduce a little, then stir in the crème fraîche and switch off the heat. Taste for seasoning and adjust accordingly.

Now for the fishballs. My son and I like this comforting kid's version: put the onion, garlic, a generous pinch of salt, and some pepper into a food processor, then pulse until well chopped. Now add the fish and semolina and pulse again a couple of times. You will end up with a homogenous, sticky mixture, but it shouldn't look too pulverized. (If you want a more adult version, finely chop the onion, garlic, and fish by hand, then add the semolina and a little beaten egg to help bind the mixture.) With wet hands, form into 10 fishballs and pop them on a plate or tray.

Heat the oil in a nonstick frying pan over medium heat and brown the fishballs, in batches, on all sides. Take care when flipping them, as they may be delicate.

Slip the browned fishballs into the tomato sauce, making sure they are submerged, and cook over low heat for 10–15 minutes, until cooked through.

Cakes, desserts, and pastries

LIFE IS SWEET

A friend from New York visited the other week. Marina Berger's family are from Odesa originally, but she was born in the Big Apple. One day, she turned around and asked me: "Olia, have you ever heard of this crazy, supposedly Ukrainian pudding called *solozhenyk*?" I almost jumped out of my chair. "Yes! The stack of pancakes covered with meringue." We started laughing, as neither of us had grown up eating it, or known of anyone making it.

On further investigation it seems that this is an old, largely forgotten recipe, consisting of thin pancakes (similar to those on page 86) spread with a lemony curd cheese and built up in layers, then topped with fruit and meringue...I can't help wondering how many more recipes like this one have all but disappeared from our repertoire.

So if not this, then what is the national Ukrainian dessert? I think it would have to be something based around curd cheese or perhaps something baked, and involving the buttery, sugary poppyseed paste that features in a lot of recipes in this chapter.

The baking book you'll find in almost every Ukrainian household is called *Solodke Pechyvo* (Sweet Bakes), by Daria Tsvek. Scanning its recipes, I see a lot of yeasted dough, kefir, curd cheese, walnuts, poppy seeds (of course!), and sour cherries, as well as some rhubarb and orange and apples. There are pancakes, sweet omelettes, and other puddings that probably made their way to Ukraine from France, via Central Europe, such as the Napoleon, a version of millefeuille.

Although it's really more of a ritual than a dessert as such, I can't resist including *kutya* here – a sweet, soupy porridge that everyone shares *before* the main Christmas meal. Of course there is another unusual dessert that Ukrainians love: dumplings filled with berries or fruit. Depending on the season, little parcels (made from the simple dough on page 174) are filled with a spoonful of fruit – sour cherries, strawberries, blackberries, bilberries, apricots, or apples – and then either boiled or steamed. There are also plum-stuffed dumplings called *knedli* that use mashed potato in the dough, which may sound weird but it works, and steamed bilberry doughnuts (*hombovtsi*) from Transcarpathia that I cannot recommend highly enough.

I hope you'll have fun making and eating the sweet things in this chapter. For a special occasion, please do give the pistachio Napoleon a go. The most luscious cake I know, it is so seductive that an English friend has christened it "boudoir baklava"!

Curd cake with caramelized apples

SERVES 8-10

---

14 Tbsp (200g) unsalted butter, softened

½ lb apples, cored and sliced

1 Tbsp brown sugar

1 cup (200g) superfine sugar (golden, if available)

3 eggs, separated

1 tsp vanilla extract

1 lb ricotta or good-quality cottage cheese

¾ cup (120g) fine semolina or polenta

Pinch of salt

My friend Jan once drunkenly asked me to cook for his dad Anton's seventieth birthday, which I (also tipsy) enthusiastically agreed to. Anton, a.k.a. Papa Florek or P Flo, grew up in Derby – his Polish father, Alfredo, had settled there after the war, when he was demobilized from the Carpathian Lancers.

Sernyk, a traditional cheesecake eaten across Poland and Ukraine, was one of Anton's childhood favorites, something that connected him to his Polish heritage, so I decided that's what I would make. Struggling to find good-quality cottage cheese the day before, I panicked and bought ricotta, adapting my mum's original recipe to suit the moister texture of ricotta. Happily, it was a huge success, and this cake is now also one of my son's favorites. I hope someone will make it for him when he is seventy.

Melt 3 tablespoons of the butter in a frying pan over medium heat, add the apples, and cook for 2–3 minutes on each side until they start to turn golden. Sprinkle in the brown sugar and cook the apples for another minute on each side, then transfer the caramelized apples to a bowl and let them cool slightly.

Preheat your oven to 400°F and grease an 8-inch square or round cake pan with butter. Lay the apples in the base of the cake pan.

If, like me, you left your butter out in the kitchen overnight, but it was so blooming cold it didn't soften properly, cut the rest of it into small pieces. Whatever state the butter is in, put it into the bowl of an electric mixer fitted with the whisk attachment, along with ¾ cup (150g) of the superfine sugar, and whisk until it's looking fairly fluffy. Break the egg yolks with a fork and gradually add them, whisking well, then whisk in the vanilla extract and cheese. Transfer the mixture to another bowl, then fold in the semolina or polenta (the latter will result in a cake with more texture).

Wash and dry your mixer bowl and whisk attachment thoroughly, then put in the egg whites and whisk until they start frothing up. Add the remaining ¼ cup (50g) of superfine sugar and the salt and keep whisking until you have soft peaks. Now take a large spoonful of the egg white mixture and fold it quite vigorously into the butter and cheese mixture to loosen it up. Add the rest of the egg white mixture and fold in gently. Pour the mixture over the apples in the cake pan and bake for 30 minutes, or until it is a little wobbly, but not liquid. Remember it will set more firmly as it cools.

Leave the cake in its pan to rest and cool down, then slice and serve. Some unsweetened tea with lemon goes perfectly with this.

Poppyseed cake with elderflower and strawberries

SERVES 8

I am not sure whose fault this is, but it seems that, in Ukraine, for eons elderflower has been thought of as coming from "the bush of the devil." Consider this passage in an old Ukrainian book called *Superstitions*: "…elder is the Devil's creation. The Devil planted it and now he forever sits under it. For this reason, so as not to tease the Devil, the elder should never be dug out with its roots, it should be left growing wherever it is. If you see an old elder stump, you should not build your house on that spot, for this is the Devil's hiding place. If you build on this spot, your children will become ill and die and your cattle will also be ill and will not procreate. If you see a young elder sapling on your vegetable patch or in your field, smother your hoe with some *salo* that has been blessed by a priest. One should not sit or lie under an elder, because one will become gravely ill."

Because of all this nonsense, even progressive people still hesitate to use elderflower in their cooking, which is a real shame as Ukraine has an enormous number of elder trees.

5 eggs, separated

1¼ cups (250g) superfine sugar

Dash of vinegar or lemon juice

2 Tbsp poppy seeds

1⅔ cups (200g) all-purpose flour

Handful of elderflower blossoms, to decorate – optional

FILLING

1⅔ cups heavy cream

½ cup (100g) superfine sugar

⅓ cup elderflower cordial

1 lb strawberries, hulled and cut into quarters

Preheat the oven to 400°F and grease an 8½-inch cake pan with a little oil or butter.

In a large bowl, whisk the egg yolks with half of the sugar until foamy and light.

In another bowl, whisk the egg whites with the vinegar or lemon juice until frothy, then gradually add the rest of the sugar and keep whisking until you have soft peaks.

Mix the poppy seeds into the flour.

Now add the egg whites to the egg yolk mixture, starting with one big spoonful to loosen the yolk mixture. Confidently fold in the rest of the egg whites apart from two large spoonfuls. Using a spatula, fold in the flour and poppy seeds, followed by the last of the egg whites. Pour the batter into the pan and bake for 40 minutes, or until a skewer inserted in the center comes out clean. Transfer the cake to a wire rack to cool.

Meanwhile, for the filling, whip the cream and sugar to soft peaks, taking care not to overwhip.

When the cake is cool, cut it in half horizontally and drizzle the elderflower cordial over the cut sides of the cake. Sandwich together with half the cream and half the strawberries, then spoon the other half of the cream over the top. Scatter with the remaining strawberries and elderflower blossoms, if using.

Potato-dough dumplings with plums and honey

SERVES 5
(MAKES 12 DUMPLINGS)

---

10 oz russet potatoes, peeled and cut into chunks

1 egg

Pinch each of salt and sugar

1¼ cups (150g) all-purpose flour

Fine semolina or polenta, for sprinkling

6 plums, halved and pitted

¼ cup brown sugar

Crème fraîche and runny honey or maple syrup, to serve

Common in western Ukraine, near the Polish border, these sweet plum dumplings most likely date back to the Austro-Hungarian Empire. They are enjoyed in many Central and Eastern European countries, and are related to the steamed doughnuts on page 300.

I realize that a potato dough with a sweet filling might seem unsettling, but I promise you will not be able to taste the potato; it just adds an amazing texture to the dough. The fruit really must deliver on flavor, otherwise this pudding might well be underwhelming, so make sure you use ripe fruit at the peak of its season. If plums are disappointing, use apricots or peaches. Blackberries or pitted cherries would also work here – use two or three per dumpling.

Cook the potatoes in a pan of salted boiling water until they are very soft, then drain and mash really well – you want the mash to be as smooth as possible.

In a bowl, mix together the egg, mash, salt, and sugar, then fold in the flour to make a wet dough. On a generously floured surface, give the dough a gentle knead, incorporating more flour to bring it all together. Wrap in plastic wrap and leave in the fridge to rest for about 20 minutes.

On a flour-dusted surface, roll the dough into a sausage shape with your hands, then cut into 12 pieces.

Sprinkle a large plate or tray with semolina or polenta. Roll out each piece of dough into a circle about 4 inches in diameter, then sit a plum half in the middle and sprinkle with a little sugar. Close the dough around the plum, pressing the edges together to make a half-moon shape, then place the dumpling, seam side down, on the plate or tray. Keep the dough and dumplings covered with a damp kitchen towel while you work, so they don't dry out.

Cook the dumplings, six at a time, in a large pan of boiling water for about 6 minutes, or until they float. Serve with crème fraîche and honey or maple syrup.

Flourless poppyseed cake

SERVES 10

Ukrainians count poppies, cornflowers, periwinkles, sunflowers, and marigolds among our national and folkloric symbols – and poppy seeds are often used in cooking, especially when it comes to baking.

When I was given this recipe by the young and brilliant head chef of Kyiv's Kanapa restaurant, Yaroslav Artyukh, I assumed it was a modern creation, but it seems that poppy seeds have been used in place of flour in the past. In *European Peasant Cookery*, Elisabeth Luard explains that poppy seeds, apart from being used for sweet strudel fillings, were "ground down into flour and used, mixed with eggs, to make a nourishing wheat-free and fat-free cake." Initially, I was unconvinced that such a cake could be delicious, but Yaroslav has cracked it, and this is now a favorite. If you want to make it dairy-free, boil the poppy seeds in 2 cups of water instead of the milk and water mix. Blackcurrants (frozen are great) are excellent with this – especially if soaked in crème de cassis liqueur for an hour or so – as is ice cream, in place of the custard.

1¾ cups (250g) poppy seeds

1 cup whole milk

1 cup (110g) confectioners' sugar

2 tsp baking powder

Finely grated zest of ½ lemon

6 eggs

2 Tbsp vegetable oil

2 egg whites

6 Tbsp (80g) superfine sugar

BAY CUSTARD

1¼ cup whole milk

10 fresh bay leaves

¼ cup (50g) superfine sugar

3 egg yolks

1 Tbsp cornstarch

Put the poppy seeds, milk, and 1 cup of water into a saucepan and simmer for 50 minutes–1 hour or until softened, adding a splash more water if it evaporates too fast. Leave to cool slightly, then transfer to a food processor and blitz to a fine paste – it will become creamier and lighter in color when it's ready. Add the confectioners' sugar, baking powder, lemon zest, eggs, and vegetable oil, then blitz until you have a smooth batter. Pour into a large bowl.

Preheat the oven to 350°F. Grease the sides of an 8-inch square cake pan with butter or oil and line the base with baking parchment, then grease the baking parchment. Whisk the egg whites to soft peaks, then gradually add the superfine sugar and keep whisking until you have stiff peaks. Confidently fold the egg whites into the poppyseed batter with a spatula. Gently pour the mixture into the pan and bake for 50 minutes, or until a skewer inserted into the middle of the cake comes out clean. Leave the cake to cool in its pan – don't worry if it sinks slightly as it cools.

Meanwhile, for the bay custard, pour the milk into a saucepan and tear in the bay leaves. Bring to a simmer, then switch off the heat and leave to infuse for about an hour. Strain out the bay leaves. Return the infused milk to the pan and bring back to a simmer. In a bowl, whisk the sugar with the egg yolks and cornstarch, then add a little of the hot milk, stirring so the eggs don't curdle. Pour back into the pan of milk and keep stirring over low heat until the custard thickens enough to coat a wooden spoon – if you drag a finger through the custard on the spoon, the trail should remain.

Cut the cake into squares and serve with the bay custard.

Pistachio Napoleon

SERVES 10

It is very inspiring to see female chefs thriving on the Ukrainian restaurant scene. Nika Lozovskaya runs Dizyngoff, in Odesa, as well as having several other projects on the go, and this recipe is hers. It is so tasty that I once ordered it three times in a row!

Pistachios add both flavor and color to this classic Napoleon (a pastry similar to a millefeuille). It can be a little fiddly to make, but the good news is that you can make the pastry sheets a couple of days in advance and then assemble the layers the day before you want to serve it, rather than stressing at the last minute.

PASTRY

2 tsp white wine vinegar

4½ cups (550g) all-purpose flour

1 tsp fine sea salt

18 Tbsp (250g) unsalted butter, cut into small cubes and chilled in the freezer

PISTACHIO CREAM

1⅓ cups (150g) pistachios or ready-made pistachio paste

6 egg yolks

1 cup (200g) superfine sugar

⅔ cup (70g) cornstarch

1 qt whole milk

1 cup heavy cream

5 Tbsp (70g) cold unsalted butter, cut into small cubes

½ cup (50g) flaked almonds, lightly toasted

Scant ½ cup (50g) pistachios, lightly toasted and roughly chopped

For the pastry, mix the vinegar with ½ cup of cold water. Put the flour, salt, and butter into a food processor and blitz until crumbly. With the machine running, slowly drizzle in the vinegar and water. When the dough starts to form clumps, turn it out onto a flour-dusted surface and knead. At first it will feel like sticky putty and you might think it will never work – but don't worry, just bring it together as best you can and roll it into a sausage shape. Cut into 10 equal pieces, then wrap each piece in plastic wrap. Chill in the fridge for at least an hour, or as long as overnight.

When you're ready to bake the pastry sheets, preheat the oven to 400°F. Have two large baking sheets and two wire racks at hand.

On a flour-dusted surface, start rolling out the first piece of pastry. It may feel a little hard to begin with, but it will relax and soften as you keep rolling. If things start to get sticky, flour the top of your pastry as well. Eventually you should end up with a thin, leathery sheet of pastry about 14 inches across. Gently lift the pastry and lay it on the back of the baking sheet.

Put it into the oven and bake for 8–10 minutes, checking after 6 minutes, just in case your oven is more ferocious than mine – it should bubble up and turn golden all over, though the first one nearly always comes out darker. Carefully remove the baking sheet from the oven – the pastry will be very fragile. Gently slide the pastry sheet onto one of the wire racks, then leave the hot baking sheet to cool down; in cold weather, I put mine outside to speed things up.

Now repeat the process with the next piece of pastry, baking it on the back of your second, cool baking sheet. Slide the second cooked pastry sheet onto the second wire rack and, when it has cooled down, stack it on top of the first pastry sheet. Keep rolling out and baking your pastry, rotating the trays and making sure each raw pastry sheet goes onto a baking sheet that is completely cool.

>>

The cooked pastry sheets will keep for at least 2 days; I just leave mine on a tray on top of the fridge, covered with a clean kitchen towel. Don't worry if some of your pastry sheets have crumbled – you can use them to decorate the sides of the cake later.

For the pistachio cream, if using nuts (rather than ready-made paste), boil them in a pan of boiling water for 5 minutes, then drain and slip off the papery brown skins. Leave to cool, then transfer to a blender or food processor and blitz to a fine paste.

In a heatproof bowl, whisk the egg yolks with the sugar, cornstarch, and ½ cup of the milk. Heat the rest of the milk and the cream in a saucepan. When it starts steaming, pour half of it into the egg yolk mixture, whisking all the time, then pour back into the pan. Cook over lowish heat, stirring constantly, until the mixture thickens – this will be pretty instant, given the amount of cornstarch.

Remove from the heat and whisk in the pistachio paste. Now gradually whisk in the cold butter, a few cubes at a time, until it is all incorporated. Let it cool down to room temperature, then press a sheet of baking parchment or plastic wrap onto the surface to prevent a skin from forming and chill in the fridge until needed.

To assemble, place one of the pastry sheets onto a serving plate or chopping board. Spread a ladleful of the pistachio cream over the pastry sheet, then place the next pastry layer on top. Keep going with these layers, finishing with a layer of pistachio cream. I like to let the Napoleon sit for a day at this point, so the pastry absorbs the pistachio cream; in my opinion that's the whole point of the pastry here – to suspend the cream in the air!

To serve, trim the edges to neaten if needed. Scatter the toasted almonds and pistachios over the top and press broken pastry (or more flaked almonds) around the sides, then cut into squares.

Steamed bilberry doughnuts

SERVES 6-8
(MAKES 15 DOUGHNUTS)

¾ cup whole milk

6 Tbsp (80g) superfine sugar

1 x ¼-oz packet fast-action
dried yeast

2 eggs, lightly beaten

1 tsp vanilla extract

Good pinch of fine sea salt

3¾ cups (450g) all-purpose
flour

2 cups (200g) walnuts, toasted
until quite dark

¼ cup (60g) brown sugar

Fine semolina, for sprinkling

8 oz bilberries (or blueberries
or other berries)

7 Tbsp melted unsalted butter

Handful of whole walnuts,
to decorate – optional

I have eaten steamed bilberry doughnuts in western Ukraine more than once – to the detriment of my waistline, but they were worth it! Filled with luscious purple fruit and dipped in toasted nuts, they were simply incredible. There is something about steamed dough that makes it irresistible. You could fill the doughnuts with the poppyseed paste on page 310 instead, if you like. And if you omit the sweet filling, the dough can also be used to make the savory garlic buns known as *pampushky* (page 158).

Warm the milk until it is lukewarm, then add 4 tablespoons (50g) of the superfine sugar and the yeast and set aside for 10–15 minutes, or until it starts frothing up. Add the eggs, vanilla, and salt, then gradually incorporate the flour. On a well-floured surface, bring the dough together by kneading it lightly – you should end up with a light, soft dough. Cover with a clean kitchen towel and leave to proof for an hour, or until doubled in size.

Using a mortar and pestle, bash the nuts with the brown sugar until coarsely crushed, then spread them out on a large plate and set aside for later.

Have ready a tray or large plate sprinkled with semolina.

Dust your worktop with flour. With well-floured hands (the dough will be sticky), take a 2-oz piece of the dough and form it into a ball. Dust the surface and dough with flour again, then use a rolling pin to gently roll it out into a 3¼-inch circle. Put a teaspoonful of bilberries and a little sprinkling of the remaining superfine sugar in the center. Fold in the edges, pulling them together and pinching firmly, then roll the doughnut between the palms of your hands into a ball.

Put the doughnut on the semolina-dusted tray or plate and repeat with the rest of the dough and berries. Cover the doughnuts with the kitchen towel and leave somewhere warm to proof for 1 hour.

Meanwhile, get a steamer ready, or use a colander set over a large saucepan of boiling water. Lightly brush the steamer basket or colander with oil. Add the doughnuts, cover, and steam for about 20–25 minutes. To check if they're done, cut one in half to make sure the dough is cooked all the way through.

Put the melted butter into a large bowl. Use tongs to dip the hot doughnuts in the butter, then roll in the crushed nuts and sugar. Top with whole walnuts, if you like, and serve warm or at room temperature.

Poppyseed, pecan, and apple strudel

SERVES 8-10

1¼ cups whole milk

⅔ cup (100g) poppy seeds

5 oz pecans, lightly toasted and roughly chopped (1¼ cups)

1 tsp vanilla extract

7 Tbsp salted butter, roughly chopped

½ cup (100g) brown sugar

3 apples, peeled, cored and cut into cubes

6 filo pastry sheets, each about 16 x 12 inches

3½ Tbsp (50g) unsalted butter, melted

1 egg, lightly beaten

Every Easter we used to wake to the smell of yeasty dough as the *makoviy rulet* baked in the oven; this poppyseed and walnut roll, a traditional Eastertime delicacy, is popular all over Ukraine.

I love working with yeasted dough, it's soft and comforting, but sadly it can also be quite time-consuming. And, let's be honest, this recipe is mostly about how much of the sweet poppyseed paste you can get into the dough – I like it to be overwhelmingly poppyseedy, you might be unsurprised to learn! So I found a way to make the process easier and quicker, without compromising on taste, by rolling up the poppyseed paste in filo pastry with some apples. Given that all kinds of strudels have made their way into Ukrainian cuisine via the Austro-Hungarian Empire, this adaptation doesn't feel out of place. After a big Easter lunch, a small slice of this with a cup of strong black coffee or tea with lemon (the traditional way to drink it in Ukraine) is heavenly.

Put the milk and poppy seeds into a saucepan and bring to a boil, then turn down to a simmer and cook for 30 minutes, adding a splash more milk if it starts looking dry. Keep an eye on it – milk tends to run away when you are not watching! When the milk has been absorbed, take off the heat and leave to cool, then transfer to a food processor. Add the nuts and vanilla, along with 6 tablespoons (80g) of the chopped butter and 6 tablespoons (80g) of the brown sugar, then blitz to a fine paste.

In a saucepan over medium heat, cook the apples in the remaining butter and sugar until softened, 5–7 minutes, then let them cool.

Preheat the oven to 400°F and lightly grease a large baking sheet with butter.

Lay 1 sheet of filo on your worktop and brush generously with melted butter, then repeat with 2 more sheets of filo, stacking them on top of the first one. Gently spread with half of the poppyseed paste, using a spoon or your hand (easiest in my opinion) and leaving a ½-inch border all around. Lay another sheet of filo on top and this time brush lightly with melted butter, concentrating on the edges. Repeat with the last 2 sheets of filo. Spread over the rest of the poppyseed paste, followed by the apples. Now use your hands to roll up the pastry into a long sausage shape, starting from one of the longer sides of the rectangle and gently tucking in the apples as you go along.

Carefully lift the strudel onto the baking sheet, placing it seam side down, and brush with beaten egg. Bake for 20–25 minutes, or until golden and crispy. Cool on the tray, then cut into small slices to serve.

Lyuba's honey and berry teacake

SERVES 8

---

3 eggs

3 Tbsp lard, softened

¾ cup (250g) runny honey

7 Tbsp whole milk

1 tsp vanilla extract

Pinch of fine sea salt

2½ cups (300g) self-rising flour

12 oz (3 cups) mixed berries (frozen is fine – defrost and drain well)

Confectioners' sugar, for dusting

Crème fraîche, to serve – optional

In the Transcarpathian village of Nyzhne Selyshche, I met a wonderful woman called Lyuba. A biology teacher, she also keeps and breeds colonies of the small and rather docile local variety of honeybee, and collects wild flowers and herbs. Her hives are designed with an extra compartment, where these herbs are dried to make herbal teas. The bees' fluttering wings help the process along, and in return, Lyuba believes, the essential oils that evaporate from the herbs as they dry help the bees stay healthy and strong. Only very limited amounts of honey are produced by Carpathian bees, so it is not a huge commercial operation.

When I visited, Lyuba made this fruit-topped teacake, and we ate it with some of her extraordinary herbal tea. It is lovely with berries, as here, but sliced apricots or peaches also work really well. If you'd rather not use lard, you can use butter, but it produces quite different results, making a drier cake.

Preheat the oven to 400°F and grease an 8-inch square cake pan.

In a large bowl, whisk the eggs and lard with the honey until foamy and light – keep scraping the bottom of the bowl, as the lard can clump there. Gradually add the milk, mixing well, followed by the vanilla and salt, to make a lumpy batter. Fold in the flour with a spatula, making sure it is fully incorporated.

Pour the batter into the pan and scatter the berries over the top. Bake for 1–1¼ hours, or until a skewer inserted in the center comes out clean. Transfer to a wire rack and leave to cool, then dust with confectioners' sugar.

This is not an overly sweet cake, and it goes brilliantly with a dollop of crème fraîche and an aromatic herbal tea sweetened with honey.

Honey cookies

MAKES 25-30 COOKIES

I've always known of *manty* (dumplings), but until recently I'd never heard of these cookies, with their cute-sounding name of *mantulky* (pronounced *mahn-tool-ky*). Prior to independence, Ukrainian wasn't taught at school until Year Two. In fact, when my parents were young, if a child spoke Ukrainian in school they were sometimes bullied and called *selyuk*, a derogatory word for "villager," so kids mostly stuck with state-imposed Russian. My parents ended up speaking mostly Russian at home, and that's why my Ukrainian is less fluent than I wish it was – although really I should no longer use that as an excuse.

My friend Katrya was far more resilient than me, however, and when she was young, she lost herself in Ukrainian literature, where she hungrily read about a character munching on one of these delectable cookies, and just fell in love with the word *mantulky*. So, when she began cooking, she was thrilled to discover the classic old cookbook called *Dishes and Drinks of Ukraine*, by Zinoviya Klynovetska. Published in 1913, this is one of those books where things are measured in buckets, and where you can find, yes, *mantulky*!

1½ Tbsp (30g) honey, agave syrup or watermelon molasses (page 66)

1 egg

7 Tbsp (100g) butter, softened

½ cup (100g) superfine sugar

2 cups (260g) all-purpose flour

½ tsp baking powder

A pinch each of ground nutmeg and allspice

4 oz mixed seeds (sunflower, sesame, poppy, pumpkin, linseed)

¼ cup (30g) dried fruit, such as sour cherries, cranberries, or raisins – optional

In a small bowl, whisk together the honey or agave syrup and egg.

In a large bowl, cream together the butter and sugar until very light and fluffy. Gradually add the honey and egg mixture, incorporating it thoroughly. Mix in the remaining ingredients to make a firm dough.

On a sheet of plastic wrap or re-usable wrap, use your hands to shape the mixture into a sausage. Wrap and chill in the fridge for 30 minutes.

Preheat the oven to 400°F. Dust two baking sheets with flour.

Unwrap the dough and cut into ¾-inch slices, then roll each slice into a ball. Place on the baking sheets and flatten sightly, then use a fork to make criss-cross marks in the top of each cookie.

Bake for 20 minutes, or until the cookies are set and golden. Transfer to a wire rack to cool.

Poppyseed babka

MAKES 2 BABKAS

In Ukraine, there is a saying that if someone can work with dough, they can communicate with spirits. Bronislava, a Polish woman who lived in a Jewish neighborhood of my hometown, was one of these people, and not one Christmas Eve or other holiday went by without her baking poppyseed *zavyvanets* (babkas). Although I never met her, I've been told that going to her house for dinner was like traveling to a different country, a different dimension. There were no carpets on the walls (a bizarre but extremely common fixture that seemed to go into decline around much the same time as the USSR did) and the table was always laid with a white linen cloth and silver cutlery.

You'll need to start this recipe the day before. It makes two babkas, but you can freeze one (or both) of them before the final proofing, ready for a rainy day.

¼ cup (50g) sourdough starter (page 154)

3¾ cups (450g) bread flour

¾ cup (100g) all-purpose flour

2 eggs, lightly beaten

¼ cup (60g) unsalted butter

¾ cup (140g) superfine sugar

1 tsp fine sea salt

1 egg white, lightly beaten

POPPYSEED PASTE

½ cup + 2 Tbsp whole milk

⅔ cup (100g) poppy seeds

6 Tbsp (80g) salted butter, roughly diced

1 cup (100g) toasted pecans

½ cup (100g) soft brown sugar

1 tsp vanilla extract

To activate your starter, put it in a bowl and add 6 tablespoons of the bread flour and ¼ cup of water. Mix well, then cover with a clean kitchen towel and leave at room temperature for 6 hours.

Now mix the all-purpose flour and ¼ cup of water into the activated starter – it should be wet to the touch, but comparatively stiff-looking. Leave, covered with the kitchen towel or plastic wrap, for about 2–3 hours somewhere warm (it may take longer than this if it's cold). The sponge is ready when it has doubled in size.

Pop your sponge and ¾ cup of water into an electric mixer fitted with the whisk attachment, and whisk until frothy, then gradually add the eggs, whisking until well incorporated. Now swap over to the dough hook attachment, add the remaining 3⅓ cups (400g) of bread flour and mix for 1 minute. The dough will look wet and gloopy. Cover and leave to rise somewhere warm for 1 hour (or longer if it's cold). When it's ready, it should look bubbly and ever so slightly risen.

Meanwhile, melt the butter in a small saucepan and stir in the sugar and salt, then let it cool down until it is barely warm. Bit by bit, start kneading the butter and sugar into the dough. I do this in the mixer with the hook attachment, but feel free to use your hands – just to embrace the slipperiness, if nothing else! When you have a smooth, shiny dough, cover and leave at room temperature overnight. (If you're making this on a hot day in summer, proof the dough in the fridge, then take it out about an hour before you want to shape it.)

>>

Next day, make the poppyseed paste. Put the milk and poppy seeds into a saucepan and bring to a boil, then turn down to a simmer and cook for 15 minutes, adding a splash more milk if it starts looking dry. Keep an eye on it – milk tends to run away when you are not watching! When the milk has been absorbed, take off the heat and leave to cool, then transfer to a food processor. Add the butter, nuts, brown sugar, and vanilla, then blitz to a fine paste.

Line two 30-ounce loaf pans with baking parchment, leaving an overhang all round to help lift out the loaves later.

The dough is ready when it's puffed up and wobbly – it will look ethereal and will feel quite wet to the touch, so make sure you flour your worktop very generously. With floured hands, gently lift the dough out of its bowl and place it tenderly on your well-floured surface. At this point, you are aiming to keep its bubbles and not deflate it too much. Flour the top of the dough and use your hands to gently press it out into a rectangle about 22 x 12 inches. Gently spread the poppyseed paste over the dough, leaving a 2-inch border all around.

Roll up the dough into a sausage shape, then cut it in half crosswise so you have two sausages of dough. Now, using a dough scraper or knife, cut one of the sausages almost in half lengthwise, to give you two lengths of dough connected at the top. Twist them, one over the other, to make a rope. Then bring the ends of the rope together, making a U-shape, and twist the ends over each other, then pinch them firmly together. You should end up with a plump-looking plait. Repeat with the other sausage of dough.

Gently lift the babkas into the loaf pans, cover with a clean kitchen towel, and leave to proof again for an hour or two, depending on how warm it is. If I am impatient, I put them on top of the mantelpiece if the fire is going, or near a radiator. But if it's cold, and you have the time, it pays to be patient as more flavor is developed during cold fermentation.

When they're ready to bake, your babkas should look risen, but not be trying to escape their pans!

Preheat the oven to 400°F. Glaze the babkas with the egg white. Pop them into the oven and bake for 30 minutes, or until golden and cooked through – when they're ready, a skewer inserted into one of the thicker parts should come out clean. Transfer the babkas to a wire rack and leave to cool.

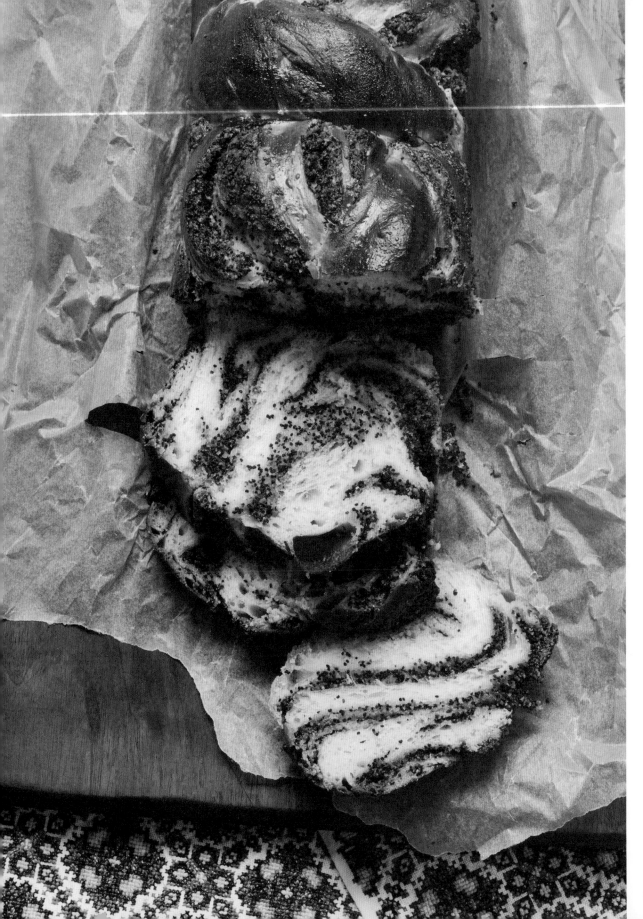

Sweet Christmas porridge

SERVES 6

In Ukraine, on the evening of 6th January, the Orthodox Christmas, a bowl of ceremonial sweet porridge, called *kutya*, is passed around the table before the pescatarian feast of twelve dishes. The word comes from either *kokkos* ("grain" in Greek) or possibly *kikkeon*, from the verb *kikkan* ("to thicken by stirring"). The dish itself dates back to pagan times. A version of it is cooked in many Eastern European countries and also in Sicily, where it is called *cuccia*, for the feast of St Lucia on 13th December.

I never really understood the appeal of this porridge when I was a child, but I always obligingly tasted it. It felt nice, all of us eating out of the same bowl. I really like the flavor now, and recognize that my warm feelings about sharing it were very appropriate, as *kutya* symbolizes compassion and reconciliation.

One of the ingredients in *kutya* is a dried-fruit-infused drink called *uzvar*, and I came across this unusual version in a village in Poltava, central Ukraine, where birch water (birch tree sap) is a

---

UZVAR

1 quart birch water or water

4 oz dried fruit, such as apricots, prunes, apples, or pears

½ cup wheat berries or pearl barley

⅔ cup poppy seeds

1 cup walnuts

1–2 Tbsp honey

To make the *uzvar*, put the birch water or water into a saucepan and add the dried fruit. Bring to a boil and simmer for around 20 minutes, then leave to cool and strain out the fruit (you can eat this with some yogurt for breakfast).

Put the wheat berries or pearl barley into a saucepan of cold water and bring to a boil, then turn down to a simmer. Wheat berries will need at least an hour; barley will take 20–30 minutes or so. Drain and leave to cool. (You can drink the barley-cooking water, by the way, and it is good for you: just add some honey, lemon, and ice.)

Put the poppy seeds into a heatproof bowl, cover with boiling water, and leave to soak for 20 minutes.

Use a mortar and pestle to crush the walnuts, but not too finely. Tip into a serving bowl.

Drain the poppy seeds, then grind to a paste with the mortar and pestle.

Mix the poppyseed paste and the wheat or barley in a serving bowl and add a little honey to taste – it shouldn't be overly sweet. Now add ¾ cup of the *uzvar* – this is just used to moisten everything, so be careful not to add too much. Pass the bowl around the table and let everyone taste a little bit.

Summer kitchen memories

While I was not able to travel to every region of Ukraine, after sending out a kind of an appeal for first-hand experiences of summer kitchens, I was fortunate enough to receive more than fifty letters. They flooded in, from across Ukraine and beyond, and from people of all ages – there were even accounts from fourth-generation Canadian Ukrainians, so vivid were the memories of summer kitchens recounted to them by their parents and grandparents.

The letters were like memory capsules, bursting with warmth and the bittersweet longing that Ukrainians call *tuga*. They were treasures that spoke of sun-soaked childhood shenanigans, berry-stained feet, and mysterious attics, the tender love of grandparents – and their occasional rebukes – and lots of life-giving, nourishing, and delicious food.

They also serve as precious historical records. As Yulia Ofutina, who now lives in Zurich, wrote of the summer kitchen that belonged to her grandparents, "…it was multifunctional. As well as preserving fruit and vegetables, grape juice was fermented there, and honey was kept in it. It was also used for frying fish, boiling crayfish, charging the car battery, distilling moonshine from honey, and boiling trotters for aspic."

I have left these accounts largely unchanged on the following pages because, expressed in their writers' own voices, they read like love letters to Ukraine, its kitchens, families, and childhoods.

Pitting cherries with a hairpin

JULIA JANCHEVSKA

I am a Ukrainian from Khmelnytsky region, but I live in New York now.

My grandparents Lyudmila and Anton had a summer kitchen in Dyavidkivtsy village, surrounded by forests, the River South Bug, and many, many ponds.

The kitchen was very spacious, with two windows, one facing the vegetable patch and the other looking into the courtyard. We had a real pich oven there and a huge cellar.

In summertime everyone sat around the large round table where we ate. We'd have a sorrel soup called kvasets, sausages, and all the buns and dumplings. The ingredients were local – in fact, most of them were homegrown in our two big vegetable gardens nearby – and we also kept rabbits, pigs, and chickens.

My whole childhood belonged to this summer kitchen, where I helped my mum and grandma do whatever needed to be done.

I have such warm memories of this time, especially when the cherries were collected and there were endless buckets of them. We had a special cherry pitter, but we still used a hairpin! It was more effective that way. We laughed a lot and fired cherry pits at each other. Thinking about it now makes me smile.

There was always a glut of everything, and our cellar was large, so preservation was taken quite seriously. Everything was saved for winter – pears, apples, strawberries, raspberries, plums, grapes, sweet and sour cherries – all were turned into jam or kompot fruit drink.

We also made kraut and fermented tomatoes, cucumbers, and large sweet peppers, which got preserved in jars. We made adjika (spicy pepper paste), tushonka (preserved slow-cooked pork), salo (cured pork fat), and sausages.

The regional name for a summer kitchen is shopa, but we also used it in winter – a couple of times we had to walk across the freezing snow to reach it – and it was where we cooked lavish Christmas and Easter feasts. The large masonry oven was there, so there was more space for all of us to cook. At Easter, we would take our food to the church to be blessed, and at Christmas it went straight to the festive table.

Every house in the village had a shopa kitchen and most of them are still around, just like ours.

Homemade butter and dried apples

OLIA RABY

I come from the Luhansk region of eastern Ukraine, but I live in Wisbech, Cambridgeshire, in the UK, now.

The summer kitchen I remember was my grandmother Tosya's, in the village of Shirokiy. It is still there and is in good condition, but as there is now a proper kitchen attached to the main house, it is mainly used as a storage space.

The summer kitchen was built by my grandad, who passed away more than twenty years ago. It was made of large clay bricks, and covered in a cement and sand mix called shuba ("fur coat"), a type of cladding used on the majority of houses in that region. The kitchen had a rather wonky window with blue wooden panels. There was one big room, with a stove in the corner. In the winter, when the kitchen wasn't in use, the stove would have a pile of pots and buckets stored on top of it. There was a table and a bed – the table was for chopping and preparing food, but I still don't know why the bed was there. My guess is that it was for when my grandad had one too many glasses of homemade wine and grandma wouldn't let him in the house!

Grandma Tosya also had another outdoor kitchen, under the shade of a big walnut tree, that was used on really hot summer days. This one was in the garden and consisted of just four posts and a roof – there were no walls and it was only big enough for a stove, table, and bench. The stove was handmade from bricks covered with a thick layer of clay. Every winter, sharp frosts would crack the clay, making it fall off in places, and every spring grandma would cover the stove with a new layer of clay. She grew everything – even the sunflower oil came from her homegrown sunflower seeds that we'd harvest and send to the mill to be processed. I can't remember her buying any food when me and my sister stayed there for the summer. All the vegetables, fruit, and meat were preserved for the winter. I remember spending ages preparing fruit for jam, and slicing apples so they could be spread out in a sunny spot to dry.

Grandma kept pigs, chickens, and a cow, and she made her own butter, cheese, and ryazhanka (fermented baked milk). I loved drinking milk fresh from the cow's udder. Grandma would put it through a sieve to get rid of any tiny flies and hairs that might have fallen into it, and pour us a glass each. And I remember watching her make butter: she'd take a three-quart jar full of cream and keep shaking it until butter was formed.

When she wanted to cook borsch, grandma would ask me and my sister to run over to the greenhouse to pick tomatoes, and to the vegetable patch for dill, onions, carrots, and potatoes. Her borsch really stood out: she would leave one potato whole and, when the soup was ready, she would fish out the potato and mash it, then put it back into the borsch to make it nice and thick. I also remember grandma's flatbreads called pyshka. She would fold the dough several times, spreading it with oil, so that when it cooked you would get lovely layers in the bread. Sometimes we'd boil corn on the cob in a massive saucepan, with a layer of green husks to cover them in the water. When it was done, we'd eat it just with some salt rubbed on it, so simple.

I wish I knew more about the cooking of my home region – if I had the chance again now, I would ask loads of questions about how everything was made.

Video-call borsch

NATALIA YATSENKO

I live in Riga, Latvia, although I grew up in Dnipro (which was then called Dnipropetrovsk), in central Ukraine.

My grandparents Maria Grigorievna and Anatoliy Nikiforovich had a summer kitchen there. They died eighteen years ago now, and the house was sold, so I have no idea if the summer kitchen is still there, but it was built of bricks, so I suppose it might be!

Grandad built the summer kitchen from scratch, using the bricks he had left over after house renovations. It was just the one room, with a small stove connected to a gas canister and a couple of tables; there were no shelves, it was mostly practical working surfaces. It was a very simple place that was mainly used by my granny – it felt like her territory. Even though my grandad cooked quite well and often, he normally cooked in the house.

My granny cooked the best omelette ever, simple but so good – it was thick but fluffy. Grandad would gather berries for me first thing, so that when I awoke there would be a plate of them waiting for me. There was also milk from the morning milking and maybe some fresh bread from the small local bakery.

I still have grandmother's handwritten recipe books. My parents cook mostly regional cuisine, and my aunt cooks only traditional local dishes. I don't, because my partner cooks well and because I am lazy! But I make borsch every few months for special occasions or when we have people round, and a couple of times a year I make varenyky dumplings.

I have a story that enthralled me as a child, and it still does today. My ancestors are from Petryakivka, which is famous for its Ukrainian folk art, and my great-grandfather had a huge cherry orchard there. It was so vast that it took the entire family to pick the cherries, and afterwards my great-grandmother would cook a feast for everyone.

One of the dishes was always a borsch containing two whole chickens, two other types of meat, and salo (cured pork fat). It was so outstanding that my father never forgot that flavor, and my mama spent twenty years attempting to reproduce it at home, using less meat to create the same taste. Eventually she succeeded, because she is a very persistent woman.

Whenever I cook borsch, I call my parents (who still live in Ukraine) and ask them for the recipe. It is mostly the same, but sometimes it varies. Of course I have it written down, but I take pleasure from them explaining it again, and my father calls me via Skype to actually look at the pot and to see how I cut the cabbage and supervise the whole process. It is very sweet.

Sausage-making and campfire potatoes

HALYNA BIGUN HILL

For the past four years I've lived in Idaho Falls, USA, but I grew up in Mariupol, eastern Ukraine. And I was actually born in Kopaihorod, in the Vinnytsia region of central Ukraine – this was my own "paradise," where my grandmother's summer kitchen was, and where I spent every summer of the 1990s.

Our family of five was struggling at the time, and it was hard to get good food in the city, so in the summertime we were sent to stay with Grandma to be fattened up. We always came back happy, healthy-looking, and rosy-cheeked, despite the fact that she let us have treats all day long – we were even allowed ice cream twice a day!

The village was predominantly Jewish, but in the 1990s a lot of people left, mainly for Israel, and Jewish villages like this one now stand bare, overgrown with wild shrubs and trees. There was a strong communal spirit. Neighbors would come and help with the slaughtering of the pig and the cleaning of the intestines – I remember how bad they smelled before that!

Our village was famous for its sausages: fried, smoked, or covered in lard to be kept over winter, all were outstanding. When I visited my family with my American husband, he loved our special local sausages, even though he is not a great meat-eater.

The summer kitchen was used to cook food for the pigs and to pluck chickens, and for family cooking, especially during the hotter months of the year. Grandma cooked traditional Ukrainian food: tiny holubtsi cabbage rolls, cooked in plenty of tomato sauce, and varenyky dumplings – savory ones filled with potato, and sweet ones with sour cherries or curd cheese. If my sisters and I were hungry before bedtime, she'd give us freshly picked strawberries covered in sugar and smetana. She also made something she called "pizza," but really it was just a delicious vegetable pie.

There were hills all around, meadows and woodland, and springwater so full of minerals that a residue settled out of it after a few days – I think this must be one of the reasons the fruit and vegetables were so delicious.

I was obsessed with potatoes, which my grandmother grew plenty of. I especially loved mashed potato with smetana and thinly sliced potatoes fried with salo and onions. One of my fondest memories was when, late one evening, my sister and I lit a fire outside, and we baked potatoes in their skins on the coals, then ate them in the summer kitchen.

Snakeskins and dried chicken stomachs

DARIA URE

I live in Reading now, in the UK. But I grew up in Yasynuvata, in the Donetsk region of Ukraine, surrounded by flat steppes. This is where my grandmother Lena had her summer kitchen. The site is currently unoccupied, because of the ongoing armed conflict with Russia in eastern Ukraine. The old house and kitchen were knocked down so my parents could build a new house, but it sits empty at the moment because of the fighting, which makes me very sad.

The summer kitchen was next to the main house, across a yard. Made out of clay and built around the wood-fired pich oven, it was mainly used for cooking in summer, but my grandmother also used the wood-fired oven during the winter.

There were lots of shelves lining the walls where plates were kept, with curtains drawn over them instead of wooden doors. There was also a side room off the kitchen, with an iron-framed bed and some other old furniture, where we used to relax after eating.

My babushka Lena had dried corn hanging from the ceiling, and she kept various preserves in tins, including dried chicken stomachs that she would give us when we had tummy ache. She also kept a dried snakeskin in a jar as a superstition; if you found a snakeskin in the woods, it was supposed to bring you luck.

In the kitchen garden, Lena grew onions, potatoes, beans, tomatoes, cucumbers, apples, strawberries, raspberries, and blackcurrants, and we preserved the berries and apples by making them into jams. She would kill a pig every year in winter (when the weather was cold, so the meat wouldn't spoil) and we would make sausages, including blood sausages and preserved meat.

When Lena made cookies in the summer, she used metal stencils to cut out shapes, and my favorite shape was the fish. Other favorites were varenyky dumplings filled with potato and onion, mashed potato with fried onions, salo roasted in the oven with garlic, and freshly caught fish.

I look back on the food of my childhood with great nostalgia, especially as I have had to leave the area where I grew up and where I spent many very happy years with my beloved family.

Even in such a globalized world, it is hard to find some of the things I used to love eating in Ukraine – especially sunflower seeds eaten straight from their shells and good dark bread. A lot of Ukrainian food was natural and less processed, and sometimes I miss that a great deal.

A secret attic and the foam from the jam pan

MARINA GETZMAN

I was born in Dunaivtsi, in Ukraine, but I live in Long Island, USA, now.

Our home region is Podilia, which is at the crossroads of western and eastern Ukraine, and there are Polish, Moldovan, German, and Jewish influences on our regional cuisine. My family was originally from Halychyna, and moved into the area in the nineteenth century, when the local landlord offered them land and employment. There were a lot of textile manufacturing facilities nearby too, where many German and Jewish immigrants worked. The landscape was full of woodland, mostly flat, with small rivers flowing into the Dniester. The summer kitchen there belonged to my grandmother, Maria Posternak. When she passed away in May 2010, my father sold the property, but I think the new family still uses the summer kitchen.

A solid brick building right next to the main house, it had three rooms with separate entrances. The largest room, on the left, was the kitchen itself. It had a large gas stove with a big red gas tank next to it, and a massive masonry oven with fascinating nooks and crannies. In theory, you could sleep on it, but in my memory that space was used for storing pickling jars. Grandma would put them on an old, thick blanket and cover them with a lighter one. Almost half the room was occupied by a full-size bed with an old-fashioned sprung bedframe, where me and my cousin Andrew would jump up and down until we got yelled at.

In her summer kitchen, grandma also kept years and years' worth of issues of Pepper, an old Ukrainian satirical magazine. On rainy days, I would spend many hours flipping the pages and looking at the sharp caricatures and cartoons lampooning both Western capitalistic ways of life and Ukrainian social issues, such as alcoholism, thievery, laziness, and parasitism.

The middle room was narrow and dark, full of random work tools that were kept under lock and key most of the time. To the right of this were three pig stalls and two rabbit cages. The pigs were way before my time; however, I do remember my grandparents keeping rabbits, and us kids collecting dandelion leaves to feed them every day in the summer. That room also had a ladder to the attic, a strange and dark place full of more old things and tools. We weren't allowed up there, but we peeked anyway, every time we got a chance. Since there was no light – and we couldn't ask for a torch, as that would lead to questioning – we only glimpsed what we could see in the dark, which wasn't much!

Next to the summer kitchen, there was a chicken coop and a fenced chicken run, so my grandmother always had fresh eggs. Sometimes she would let me collect them. On special occasions, a chicken would be killed, and then we had the most delicious chicken soup, with amber yellow broth and homemade noodles.

My grandma made the best pyrizhky buns, filled with poppy seeds, apples, or sour cherries, but my favorite thing to eat was sour cherry preserves. Grandma's strawberry preserves were also outstanding – I loved the sweet, sugary foam from the giant enamel jam pan where the berries were slowly cooked for hours before being canned. She would skim it off into a porcelain saucer so I could eat it later on, when it had set.

Rhubarb buns and hailstorms

SOFIA VOZNIUK

I am a schoolgirl, and the summer kitchen I remember is in Laskiv village, in the Volyn region of Ukraine, far from any main roads.

It is my great-grandmother's and granny's kitchen, and it is made from red bricks. Inside, the walls and ceiling are white, and the floor is wooden. There is a small entrance hall, where little chickens usually live in the summer, and another bigger room. On one side there is an old oven made from sand-lime brick and a long bench, and on the other side there's the oven, washing machine, some shelves, and a washbasin. There is also a window on that wall, with a radio on the windowsill that is always talking. On the shelves, there are different teas and cups, and in the kitchen cabinet are forks, knives, and spoons, salt and other supplies. Sparrows have made their nest near the drainpipe outside the kitchen. Also there are always lots of spiders inside.

Separated from the kitchen by a narrow pathway, the main house is used only for sleeping – though I guess the fridge is there! But it is the summer kitchen that is used for cooking food for the family. Next to the summer kitchen, we have a garage, and a barn that's used as a cowshed and pigpen. Right by it all is our vegetable patch. We also have a bigger garden a short walk away.

As the village is located near Poland, there are many borrowed words in the local dialect, and the food is also influenced by the neighboring country. There is one village dish that is special – sweet yeasted buns filled with rhubarb. Rhubarb is sour, so some sugar is added to make it tastier, and the bun tops are brushed with beaten egg using cockerel feathers. The flour is ground from homegrown wheat, so the dough is very good.

Ox tongue and boiled egg in aspic is popular too, but perhaps these are also found elsewhere in Ukraine. Another dish is called kyshka (intestine) – sausage casings stuffed with a mixture of salo (cured pork fat), potato, and buckwheat.

We have varenyky dumplings, too, filled with potatoes or offal, or with sour cherries and bilberries for pudding. Then you pour…no, you spoon soured cream called smetana on them. In fact, you have to scrape it off the spoon with another spoon, as it is homemade, not from the shops, so it is very thick! Another unusual dish is chocolate kysil, which is like a cocoa jelly made with cornstarch.

When guests come, the table strains under the weight of all the dishes. There are always at least two salads, fish fried in egg batter, some meat (either chicken or duck), and meat-stuffed bagels – these are tricky to make, and it takes some skill to stuff the bagel's hole with meat. They are then soaked in milk and coated in breadcrumbs before being deep-fried. For dessert, there is a cake or some cookies shaped like nuts, and we'll drink birch water or a plum and apple kompot.

My brightest memory of the place comes from a summer's day. It had started to hail, and everyone gathered in the summer kitchen. The big dog was lying on the floor, five cats were sleeping on the bench. My granny was cooking something for supper. I was sitting and listening to the radio. After the hail, the sun came out and the view of the garden from the window was enchanting.

Menu suggestions

A MIDSUMMER FEAST

Fish broth with dill and garlic *lyok* (p.138)
-
Zucchini with herbaceous *lyok* dressing (p.210)

Cabbage and cucumber salad (p.214)

Tomato and mulberry salad (p.206)

Young garlic scapes in butter (p.234)

Panfried turbot (p.278)
or
"Black swan effect" peppers stuffed with
apple, carrot, and rice (p.222)
-
Poppyseed cake with elderflower and
strawberries (p.288)

AN AUTUMN COOKOUT

Sashko's *bogracz* stew (p.260)
or
Vegetable casserole (p.226)
-
Fermented Gagauz stuffed peppers (p.30)

Raw turnip and green onion salad with
yogurt dressing (p.204)

Potato cakes stuffed with bean and feta paste
(p.240)
-
Curd cake with caramelized apples (p.286)

A COZY FAMILY MEAL

Southern borsch with a giant dumpling (p.136)
or
Mushroom broth with sour pickles (p.144)
-
Fishballs in tomato sauce (p.280) – with mash
or
Pot-roast chicken cooked in herby crème
fraîche (p.256)

Apple, celery, and kraut salad (p.208)
-
Lyuba's honey and berry teacake (p.304)

A CHRISTMAS FEAST

Sweet Christmas porridge (p.314)
-
Christmas borsch with mushroom
dumplings (p.126)
-
Slow-roast pork with kraut and dried
fruit (p.262)
or
Barley, bean, and mushroom casserole (p.224)
Dumplings with beans and potato (p.174)
Sourdough garlic buns (p.158)
-
Honey cookies (p.308)

AN EASTER LUNCH

Eggs with horseradish mayonnaise
and wild garlic (p.108)

Ukrainian blood sausage (p.266)

Whipped garlic *salo* on rye (p.102)
or
Odesan *zakuska* (p.104)

Curd cheese with green onions,
herbs, and radishes (p.98)
-
Nettle, sorrel, and wild garlic soup (p.128)
-
Lyusia's goat and onion stew with
creamy mash (p.264)
or
Lazy dumplings with green beans,
poppy seeds, and crispy shallots (p.176)
-
Poppyseed babka (p.310)

Ingredients

In my cooking I use seasonal, high-quality ingredients grown by people who care. Such ingredients might seem expensive, but remember that they take a lot of resources (time, effort, and wages) to produce, and they will help you to make nutritious dishes that deliver in terms of health benefits and flavor.

BRYNZA/VURDA CHEESE

This sheep's and/or goat's milk cheese is found in western Ukraine, in areas near the Romanian border. Softer than halloumi, with a similar springy bite, some versions of it can be quite milky and plain, but it's the salty brined stuff I love. A mixture of good feta and halloumi works quite well instead, or just feta – whenever in doubt, feta does the job.

BUCKWHEAT

Raw, green buckwheat was commonly used in Ukraine before the Soviet authorities clocked that buckwheat could be stored for much longer if it was toasted. And, frankly, this is one of the few positive things that came out of their meddling in food production, for toasted buckwheat tastes more flavorsome. If you can only get hold of the green stuff, spread it over a baking sheet and toast in a preheated 350°F oven for 15 minutes, or until the buckwheat is light brown.

BUTTER

If a recipe contains a reasonable amount of butter, please use good-quality butter, even in baking – it doesn't have to be the fancy fermented stuff. Most supermarkets stock good organic butter. Truth be told, the butter in Ukraine, unless it has been made at home and sold at a local market, is sadly not so good. My parents actually stock up on the British and French stuff whenever they visit and take it back to Ukraine. Honestly, they take fifteen packs away with them and stash it in the freezer. They put cold thick cuts of it, like cheese, on rye bread – something I highly recommend.

CREAM

Please use the best dairy products you can get hold of: full-fat and organic is best. I used to worry about the amount of cream, butter, and cheese in Ukrainian food, but now I accept that it is part of our gastronomic identity, and I will not apologize for it. *Smetana*, a type of thick, full-fat sour cream, is used extensively. In my experience, French crème fraîche is the best substitute – but if you know of a good producer of sour cream of any kind, go for it.

DRIED SMOKED PEARS AND PRUNES

Traditionally these are simultaneously dried and smoked in *pich* wood-fired ovens. Smoked prunes are pretty ubiquitous throughout Ukraine, while smoked pears are more common in Poltava and Khmelnytsk, in central Ukraine. If you ever visit Kyiv, you'll be able to find them at the large food markets, such as Zhitnii or Besarabsky. And if you want to try making your own dried smoked pears, there's a recipe on page 62.

FLOUR

If you try the sourdough recipes – and I really hope you do! – you'll need organic flour, in order to create something alive. I currently use organic flours from the online suppliers on pages 340–1, but I am also saving up for a grain mill, so I can grind my own organic wheat, spelt, and rye flour.

GARLIC

I try to buy European and, even better, locally grown garlic, rather than the Chinese stuff you often see in supermarkets. For recipes where garlic is an important ingredient, such as those that include the garlic and herb pastes known as *lyok*, please use good garlic.

MEAT

Like people of the past – and, increasingly, of the present – I try not to eat much meat. I do this for the sake of the environment and for my own health, and also because my husband is vegetarian. When I do buy meat, I go for good-quality, ethically reared meat – organic, where possible. I use a lot of offal, too, and try my best to encourage people to cook with it. My hope is that, with time, offal, including pig's trotters, ears, and tripe, as well as some of the less popular meats, such as goat, will become more readily available and more widely enjoyed.

SALO

Salo is mostly salt-cured pork fat, often with a thin strip of meat running through it, and it may also be smoked.

The basic recipe involves taking a piece of pork back fat with its skin attached and making a couple of incisions in it, without cutting into the skin, then pushing salt deep into the incisions and all over the fat. It is then left to cure on a wooden or wire rack (to allow the liquid to drain away) in a cool place.

After a couple of days the salt is washed off and the fat can then be kept in the cellar for a long time. Any older *salo* that becomes too strong to be consumed on its own can be pounded with garlic and stirred into borsch, to intensify the flavor. If you don't want to cure your own *salo*, I recommend substituting Italian *lardo* – or, if the recipe only uses *salo* as a medium for frying other ingredients, smoked pancetta.

SALT

Most people in Ukraine use table salt, as sea salt is way too expensive, but I admit to being an addict of the flaky sea salt that is harvested in foggy Albion (as we call Britain in Ukraine!), and so that is what I've used for most recipes in this book. You can use any sea salt, including the finer-grained sort, but please also follow your instincts – everyone's taste buds are different. Having said that, what I do find is that people are often scared of salt and tend to under-season. Trust me, seasoning will really bring out the flavors of the food, so if you've used good-quality ingredients but your dish tastes bland, try adding an extra pinch of salt.

SOUR CHERRIES

Sour cherries can be picked in the streets of my hometown in Ukraine. In fact, they fall on your head and stain your sandaled feet as you walk along. For many years, I struggled to find sour cherries in the UK, but you can now buy them frozen online – suppliers are listed on pages 340–1.

SUGAR

I struggle with this one. I am trying to use less and less of the refined stuff, and I did test the cake and dessert recipes in this book with organic unrefined coconut sugar, but a lot of them simply didn't work. Wherever it didn't compromise the flavor and texture, I have substituted refined sugar with honey, but I am afraid most of the cakes only work the way they should if refined sugar is used. Just remember that cake is a treat, and then let yourself have a slice occasionally; I know I do.

SYR CURD CHEESE

So important is this cheese to Ukrainians, that all other cheeses go by the same name, *syr*. Somewhere between ricotta and cottage cheese, *syr* is thicker than ricotta and more grainy, but its grains are finer than cottage cheese and it is less dry. I have adapted some recipes that usually use *syr* to use ricotta. However, for those where *syr* is a main ingredient, such as the curd cheese with green onions, herbs, and radishes (page 98), I think making your own is the way to go. Don't worry, it is much easier to make at home than you might think.

Start with 2 quarts of unhomogenized or raw milk. Pour it into a lidded jar and leave it in a warm place to go sour. Check it after 24 hours – the milk should look curdled, but smell pleasantly sour, not rank. When the milk has soured and thickened, place an empty cardboard egg carton in the bottom of a large, tall saucepan (to protect the base of the jar from the heat of the pan) and stand the jar of soured milk on top of it. Fill the pan with water so it reaches as far up the jar as possible. Bring to a boil, lower the heat, and simmer for an hour or until the whey separates out and you can see cracks forming in the curds. Wearing oven gloves, carefully lift out the jar and leave to cool slightly on a wire rack.

Meanwhile, set a cheesecloth-lined sieve over a large bowl and, while the curds are still warm, tip them into the sieve to drain. Gather the cheesecloth around the curds and tie into a bundle, then suspend it from the kitchen tap overnight, with the bowl placed underneath to catch the whey. Place the drained curd cheese (you should end up with 11–14 ounces) into a clean container with a lid and keep in the fridge for up to a week.

Don't discard the whey: you can use it to make the Ukrainian wedding bread on page 160, or the flatbreads on page 166 – or instead of water when making sourdough bread.

UNREFINED SUNFLOWER OIL
Produced simply by pressing large quantities of toasted sunflower seeds, this nutty oil was actually used for frying in Ukraine decades ago, as the refined stuff wasn't available, and my father still has unpleasant memories of it! But, used as a finishing oil, it is wonderful. The oils sold in Ukraine are very powerful in flavor, as potent as sesame oil; British and French versions I have tried are milder, but they are still good. Otherwise, pumpkin seed oil or a fresh walnut oil make good substitutes.

VEGETABLES
If you are able to use fruit and vegetables that have not been sprayed with chemicals, please do. And try to cook as seasonally as possible. Most Ukrainian dishes do not have any spices or other embellishments to hide behind – it is all about good ingredients, the stuff grown in summer kitchen vegetable patches and herb gardens. With these traditional recipes, using the freshest seasonal vegetables will make all the difference.

VINEGAR
I often call for good-quality vinegar in my recipes. There are quite a few excellent raw vinegars around these days and they're definitely worth trying for dressings, where you'll really notice the difference, but I wouldn't stress too much over small amounts of vinegar in other recipes – just use one you like.

Suppliers

ABEL & COLE

abelandcole.co.uk

A supplier of pork knuckle, offal, beef, lamb and fish. And vegetables, of course.

BELAZU

belazu.com

Mediterranean and Middle Eastern ingredients that will also work in many of the recipes in this book.

CABRITO

cabrito.co.uk

As a by-product of the dairy industry, male goats would usually be euthanized shortly after birth. Ex-River Cottage chef James Whetlor deemed this unacceptable and so he set about making kid goat meat popular. Do give it a go – it is a tender and very mild meat.

CANNON AND CANNON

cannonandcannon.com

For all your cured meat needs, including smoked pork belly, pay a visit to this brilliant online shop.

CLEARSPRING

clearspring.co.uk

It makes me happy that this family-run company's products are stocked by many supermarkets. Their range includes excellent organic unrefined and frying sunflower oils, which are so essential to Ukrainian cooking.

EVERSFIELD ORGANIC

eversfieldorganic.co.uk

I get my pork knuckle from this supplier, as well as ox heart and tongue.

FARMDROP

farmdrop.com/london

This is my go-to site for meat, fish, vegetables and dairy. They only deliver to the London area at the moment, but are hoping to extend this in future.

GILCHESTERS ORGANICS

gilchesters.com

This supplier does great stoneground heritage grain flours, as well as organic unbleached white flour.

HODMEDOD'S

hodmedods.co.uk

I often use Hodmedod's brilliant British-grown green or yellow split peas, as well as their other pulses, grains and flours.

HOOK & SON

hookandson.co.uk

If you want to make your own fermented baked milk, *ryazhanka* (page 64), or the Ukrainian curd cheese called *syr* (pages 338–9), you can order raw milk from this supplier. They also do excellent yogurt, raw butter and clarified butter.

THE MARKET GARDEN

themarketgarden.co.uk

For frozen organic sour cherries, beet with leaves on and much more.

NATOORA

ocado.com

Some Natoora vegetables and fruit can be ordered from Ocado. I get their French Goldrush apples, which are similar to some Ukrainian varieties, to use for ferments.

NEAL'S YARD DAIRY

nealsyarddairy.co.uk

Neal's Yard offer fantastic butter, crème fraîche, cottage cheese and ricotta – and their other cheeses are second to none.

PIPERS FARM

pipersfarm.com

This supplier has excellent chicken, duck, beef and Saddleback pork, including trotters, pig's ears and good-quality lard.

RIVERFORD

riverford.co.uk

An excellent supplier of organic veg boxes and great-quality meat and dairy.

SHIPTON MILL

shipton-mill.com

I get a lot of my flour, including whole-grain rye, from the online shop of this excellent supplier.

VINEGAR SHED

vinegarshed.com

The best vinegars, including my favorite blackcurrant vinegar, can be bought from this supplier, as well as olive oils, spices and preserves.

Acknowledgments

First of all, I would like to thank Bloomsbury Publishing for giving me the opportunity to write about my beloved Ukraine, its food and people. Not every author is lucky enough to be able to travel to the country they write about and to shoot there, but you have made it possible, turning this project into something very special and magical.

Thank you, Lisa Pendreigh, for fatefully kickstarting this project and for being here for the end of it. Richard Atkinson, thank you for holding fort in the middle. Natalie Bellos, thank you for seeing it through at its busiest – you have been amazing, and you will be missed very much. Xa Shaw Stewart – thank you for being a constant, for your sound advice, organization, and also warmth.

Alison Cowan, I could not have wished for a better editor, thank you for helping my writing sound so much more elegant without taking away my voice. Sarah Greeno, your design is timeless and you are one of the loveliest people I've had the pleasure to work with. Kitty Stogdon, thank you for doing the mammoth task of organizing the hundreds of photos and for so much more.

To everyone else at Bloomsbury who I may have not worked as closely with on a day-to-day basis, I very much appreciate all your hard work.

Ariella Feiner, it has now been five years. You are the best agent imaginable, thank you for always putting my integrity as a writer first. Aoife Rice, Molly Jamieson, and everyone else at United Agents, I feel so lucky that you have had my back for so many years now. Here's to many more...

Elena Heatherwick, thank you for being so enthusiastic about this project six years ago and for injecting so much enthusiasm into it. Your photographs have brought so much soul, sensitivity, and feeling into the book.

Joe Woodhouse, your food and travel photography is outstanding – thank you for putting so many more hours into this project than a photographer should ever be expected to. I am so lucky to have had you working with me on this.

Anastasia Stefurak, I really wanted to involve someone from Ukraine in the design of the book, and your work and sunny personality were simply perfect for it. Thank you for distilling the essence of *Summer Kitchens* into one perfect piece of art.

A very special, massive thank you goes to everyone in Ukraine who helped us on our journeys. I am not including names here as I worry I will inadvertently miss someone out, but you know who you are. Thank you for inviting us into your homes and enduring all my peculiar questions about forgotten recipes, masonry ovens, and childhood memories. This book simply would not have been possible without you, and the depth and warmth of your hospitality has been overwhelming.

Special thanks to all the people who took time to answer my interview questions that got turned into essays. I have read every one of them, and smiled and cried – I wish I could have included all sixty of them in the book. These essays, snippets of personal history, turned *Summer Kitchens* into something extremely special.

To Katrya Kalyuzhna, thank you for being so generous with all your knowledge, stories, and recipes. I hope someone will finally get you to write a book on Ukrainian cuisine for publication in Ukraine – we all need it!

Julia Aurora Ogorodnyk, thank you for connecting me with so many wonderful food writers and chefs all over Ukraine.

Thank you to Nika Lozovskaya and her gorgeous mother, grandmother, and sisters in Odesa, for all your recipes and stories. Olia Stepanushko and Vadym Tselukh, thank you both for everything, and for moving Odesa's gastronomic world forward.

Chef and friend, Yaroslav Artyukh, your talent astounds me, please keep bringing Ukrainian cuisine to its apogee; I expect to see you on Netflix soon.

Marianna Dushar, thank you for enlightening me about the rich and delicious Halychyna cuisine, and for your time in Lviv with brilliant Kostyantyn Kovalyshyn.

A special thank you to Ivan and Alla Plachkov for your hospitality and time. Also to Nataliya Chaneva, and sisters Mariya Chaneva and Anna Mircheva – you made the book so much more beautiful with your electric energy.

And thanks to Elena Shcherban for your expert knowledge on the history of borsch. The work you do in Poltava is invaluable.

Nataliya Cummings, thank you for your friendship, and for helping me with border connections in Transcarpathia, Rakove, and Belarus. You are the best, most natural fixer.

Sasha Lipchey, you have helped so much and brought so much positivity to our journey. Your *bogracz* recipe is the best, we keep cooking it in a *kotlich* outside, even in winter!

Irina and Aleksey Tsvelykh, thank you for your love and support and for connecting us with Serhiy Sokolovsky, driver and fixer extraordinaire, who took us on a hunt for recipes all around Poltava and Dnipro.

Huge thanks to all of my brilliant recipe testers – Isa Ouwehan, Sean Freer, Sarah Eden, Beth Osborne, Beth Hinde, Henrietta Inman, Alice Power, and anyone else I might be forgetting here. Caroline Parry and family – thank you for testing, for eating, for reading… so happy and proud that sourdough-making has become a regular activity in your house.

Thank you, Nigella Lawson, Elisabeth Luard, and Magnus Nilsson, for your beautiful quotes. Your support means a lot, and you are an ongoing source of inspiration to me.

To my super-talented mum, Olga, for always being there for us. I want to be like you when I grow up. Also, thank you for cooking and styling the photographs for the sourdough bread, Lyusia's goat stew, and southern borsch – you are a natural. Also to Dad, Aunt Lyuda and Valya, cousin Alyonka, and the rest of my extended family, thank you for everything you have done for this book (so, so much!) and for instilling in me a love and fascination for storytelling. To my older brother Sasha, thank you with all my heart for taking us to both the correct and incorrect Kosmach villages for the last leg of our insane journey. I hope we can do more research trips together soon!

Finally, on a personal level, to my husband Joe and my eldest son Sasha, I couldn't have done this without you. You are the everyday fabric of my life and a bottomless source of positivity that gives me strength and keeps me going.

Index

fraîche 256
salted herbs for winter 60
whipped garlic *salo* on rye 102
Hill, Halyna Bigun 325
honey 18
honey cookies 308
Lyuba's honey and berry teacake 304
potato-dough dumplings with plums and honey 290
hops 149
horseradish
beet and horseradish 61
eggs with horseradish mayonnaise and wild garlic 108
Hutsul people 149, 194, 200
Hutsul polenta 236

I

Ilf, Ilya 276
ingredients 337–9
Ivano-Frankivsk 28

J

jam 329
Janchevska, Julia 319
Jansson, Tove 280

K

kabytsya 247
Kadyr, Amina 170
Kagayeva, Vera 198
Kakhovka 7, 149, 154, 210
Kaliningrad 115
Kalyuzhna, Katrya 48, 154
Kamchatka 115
kefir
dumplings 136
fried flatbreads with cheese 166
Transcarpathian buns with mushrooms 168
Kherson 25, 119, 138
kimchi 77
Klynovetska, Zinovia 92, 134, 204, 308
knedli 285
kolduny 168
Komarnytsky, Bohdan 180
Kopaihorod 325
korovai 160–3
Kotliarevsky, Ivan 44
Kovalyshyn, Kostyantyn 98
Kovardiuk, Nadezhda (Nadya) 248, 251
kraut
apple, celery, and kraut salad 208
mushroom dumplings 126–7
sauerkraut with whole cabbage leaves 28–9
slow-roast pork with kraut and dried fruit 262
sour cabbage leaf rolls with pork and barley 258
spelt dumplings with kraut and caramelized onions 172–3

krovyanka 245
krstachky 166
Krynychne 18
kulesha 236
kuleshnyk 134
kutya 285, 314
kvas
beet *kvas* 68, 74, 116
chicken broth with bran *kvas*, noodles, mushrooms and lovage 140
wheat bran and polenta *kvas* 67
Kvitka, Hryhory 44
Kyiv 21, 46, 50, 115, 160, 292

L

lamb
Sashko's *bogracz* stew 260–1
spring lamb broth 130
Laskiv 331
lazy dumplings with green beans, poppy seeds and crispy shallots 176
leeks
nettle, sorrel, and wild garlic soup 128
pig's ears with garlic and paprika 270
Lindgren, Astrid 280
Lipchey, Sashko 260
lovage
chicken broth with bran *kvas*, noodles, mushrooms and lovage 140
fermented chiles 32
Lozovskaya, Nika 296
Luard, Elisabeth 17, 180, 183, 292
Lviv 18, 21, 98, 144, 172, 180, 206, 230
lyapuny 92
lyok dressing 210
fish broth with dill and garlic *lyok* 138
Lyshnynka 248
Lyuba's honey and berry teacake 304
Lyubymivka 77
Lyusia 258, 264
borsch 113, 116, 119, 120
Lyusia's goat and onion stew with creamy mash 264

M

makoviy rulet 302
manja 198
mantulky 308
mayonnaise
dill and garlic mayonnaise 192
eggs with horseradish mayonnaise and wild garlic 108
Odesan *zakuska* 104
meat 191, 242–71, 338
see also lamb; pork, *etc*
medyanyky 160
menus 335
milk, fermented baked 64
millet: fish broth with dill and garlic *lyok* 138
mint: sour eggplant with mint and chile 48
mizeria 196

weldon**owen**

Weldon Owen International
1150 Brickyard Cove Road, Richmond, CA 94801
www.weldonowen.com

First published in Great Britain in 2020 by BLOOMSBURY PUBLISHING

Text © Olia Hercules, 2020

Photographs © Elena Heatherwick, 2020: pages 1, 2, 4, 6, 10, 12, 13,
14–15, 16, 20, 34, 35, 56, 72, 75, 76, 78, 79, 80, 81 (left), 117, 118, 123, 125,
181, 182, 184, 186, 187, 202, 203, 249, 250, 252, 254, 274–5, 284, 294,
295, 316, 318, 322, 330, 334, 344

Photographs © Joe Woodhouse, 2020: pages 9, 19, 24, 27, 29, 31, 33, 37,
39, 41, 43, 45, 47, 49, 51, 55, 57, 63, 65, 69, 71, 81 (right), 84, 87, 89, 90–1,
93, 95, 97, 99, 100, 101, 103, 105, 107, 109, 112, 114, 121, 122, 124, 127, 129, 131,
133, 135, 137, 139, 141, 143, 145, 148, 151, 153, 155, 159, 161, 163, 165, 167, 169, 171,
173, 175, 177, 178, 185, 190, 193, 195, 197, 199, 201, 205, 207, 209, 211, 213, 215,
217, 219, 220–1, 223, 225, 227, 229, 231, 233, 235, 237, 239, 241, 244, 246,
253, 255, 257, 259, 261, 263, 265, 267, 269, 271, 273, 277, 279, 281, 287, 289,
291, 293, 297, 299, 301, 303, 305, 306, 307, 309, 311, 313, 315, 320, 324, 326,
328, 332–3, 336

Illustrations © Anastasia Stefurak, 2020

Olia Hercules, Elena Heatherwick, Joe Woodhouse and Anastasia Stefurak
have asserted their right under the Copyright, Designs and Patents Act,
1988, to be identified as author, photographers and illustrator,respectively,
of this work.

Extract on pages 1 and 150 from *A Russian Journal* by John Steinbeck,
published by Penguin. Reproduced by permission of The Random House
Group Limited © 1948 John Steinbeck.

Extract on page 115 from *Memories: From Moscow to the Black Sea* by
Teffi, published by Pushkin Press. Reproduced by permission of Pushkin
Press © Agnés Szydlowski, 2016. English translation © Robert Chandler,
Elizabeth Chandler, Anne Marie Jackson and Irina Steinberg, 2016.

For legal purposes the Acknowledgments on pages 342–3 constitute an
extension of this copyright page

Library of Congress Cataloging-in-Publication data is available.

ISBN: 978-1-68188-570-4

10 9 8 7 6 5 4 3

Printed and bound in China.

North American Edition
Editor Amy Marr
Art Director Bronwyn Lane